# STRESS MANAGEMENT

DR. MUKTA GOYAL DR. SAVITA MISHRA

# Contents

# Preface

In modern life, stress is a common problem for everyone. Everyone faces different types of stresses at different phases of life. Students are not the exception of this. At home, they are criticized by their parents on the basis of comparison to others and at school they suffer from study and exam pressure. The key factor of this stress is competition. In the upper classes, students face the stress from unemployment. Many students who are preparing themselves for government jobs for 5 – 6 years but don't achieve anything, are the common victims of depression. The term "Survival of the fittest" now become a stress enhancer for everyone. If you want to survive, you have to win the race and these lines destroy our daily life and health. There is a wide range of resources and strategies for dealing with pressure, just as there is a wide range of stresses. Some students meditate or listen to music to relieve stress, while others use the 4A's (avoid, alter, accept, and adapt) to overcome stress. People will cope well and will not feel as if the pressure is affecting them negatively.

Stress among adolescents is a very common phenomenon that gives rise to various issues related to both the growth and development of the body. The transitional phase shows the stage of development where the influx of stress and its responsiveness varies within individuals. The socio-economic, demographic, cultural contexts of the society indulge in the development of stress where the academic scenario with performance level either increases or decreases the level of stress.

Thus, the key function for the development of stress is the human-made factors that give rise to the dysfunctional imbalances further inculcating the immune system of the body which disturbs the mental health and the well-being of the transitional group. Thus, measures and initiatives should be considered to overcome the stressful condition where academicians, parents, peers, and counsellors should play a vital role. The development of stress if not minimized at the primary stage shall cause a psychological disturbance in the later phase of life when the adolescents would enter adulthood. Preventive measures that have been implemented to reduce stress have been evaluated and looked into, and measures that include the management of stressed-out workers and their total recovery from stress have also been analyzed.

Dr. Mukta Goyal

# PREFACE

Dr. Savita Mishra

# CHAPTER ONE

# Understanding Stress At Various Levels

**INTRODUCTION**

We all face different challenges and obstacles, and sometimes the pressure is hard to handle. When we feel overwhelmed or unsure how to meet the demands placed on us, we experience stress. In small doses, stress can be a good thing. It can give you the push you need, motivating you to do your best and to stay focused and alert. Stress is what keeps you on your toes during a presentation at work or drives you to study for your exam when you'd rather be watching TV. But when the going gets too tough and life's demands exceed your ability to cope, stress becomes a threat to both your physical and emotional well-being.

**Stress** is a psychological and physiological response to events that upset our personal balance in some way. When faced with a threat, whether to our physical safety or emotional equilibrium, the body's defenses kick into high gear in a rapid, automatic process known as the "fight-or flight" response. We all know what this stress response feels like, heart pounding in the chest, muscles tensing up, breath coming faster, and every sense on red alert.

Stress is a normal reaction to everyday pressures, but can become unhealthy when it upsets your day-to-day functioning. Here's the best science available on what happens to your body when stress hits and how to keep your stress at healthy, manageable levels.

High stress related to coronavirus is the new normal for many parents, the latest Stress in America survey finds. Nearly half of parents of children under age 18 say their stress levels related to the coronavirus pandemic are high. The COVID-19 pandemic has altered every aspect of American life, from health and work to education and exercise. Over the long term, warns the American Psychological Association, the negative mental health effects of the coronavirus will be serious and long-lasting.

**Health problems caused or exacerbated by stress include:**

1. Depression and anxiety
2. Pain of any kind
3. Sleep problems
4. Autoimmune diseases
5. Digestive problems

1. Skin conditions, such as eczema
2. Heart disease
3. Weight problems
4. Reproductive issues
5. Thinking and memory problems

**Stress Warning Signs and Symptoms**
**Cognitive Symptoms**
- Memory problems • Indecisiveness
- Inability to concentrate • Trouble thinking clearly
- Poor judgment • Seeing only the negative
- Anxious or racing thoughts • Constant worrying
- Loss of objectivity • Fearful anticipation

**Emotional Symptoms**

- Moodiness • Agitation

- Restlessness • Short temper
- Irritability, impatience • Inability to relax
- Feeling tense and "on edge" • Feeling overwhelmed
- Sense of loneliness and isolation • Depression or general unhappiness

- **Physical Symptoms**

- Headaches or backaches • Muscle tension and stiffness
- Diarrhea or constipation • Nausea, dizziness
- Insomnia • Chest pain, rapid heartbeat
- Weight gain or loss • Skin breakouts (hives, eczema)

• Loss of sex drive • Frequent colds

**Behavioral Symptoms**

• Eating more or less • Sleeping too much or too little

• Isolating yourself from others • Procrastination, neglecting responsibilities

• Using alcohol, cigarettes, or drugs to relax • Nervous habits (e.g. nail biting, pacing)

• Teeth grinding or jaw clenching • Overdoing activities (e.g. exercising, shopping)

• Overreacting to unexpected problems • Picking fights with others

**Sources of Stress**

The top four sources for stress are:

1. Money
2. Work
3. Family responsibilities
4. Health Concerns

These four categories have been the same top reasons for stress in the same order since 2008, the beginning of the recession. While the overall trend of stress levels has decreased since peaking in 2010, a deeper dive reveals some enlightening facts about Americans and their stress.

**Money: The root of all stress?**

When respondents were asked how their stress over money has changed over the past year, **88% answered that their stress has either stayed the same or increased**. So while some of the anxieties from the recession have subsided, the vast majority of Americans are still concerned about their finances. The three most significant sources of money related stress were: paying unexpected expenses, paying for essentials, and saving for retirement.

All four categories can be seen as being influenced by one another. For example, money concerns can influence decisions about health concerns, or work concerns can influence stress about family responsibilities. In fact, the APA states in their report that "Nearly 1 in 5 Americans say that they have either considered skipping or skipped going to the doctor in the past year when they needed health care because of financial concerns."

**Generation gap**

It might seem obvious that different generations would have different stresses due to their stations in life, but viewing stress through the prism of generations allows for a clearer picture of the future of stress and stress management.

The APA report highlights the divide between the generations using statistics about money stress: "Money is a somewhat or very significant source of stress for the majority of Americans (64 percent) but even more so for parents (77 percent), Millennials (75 percent) and Gen Xers (76 percent)."

**Daily Hassles and Demands**

While major life changes are stressful, they are also relative rarities. After all, it's not every day that you file for divorce or have a baby. However, you may battle traffic, argue with your family members, or worry about your finances on a daily basis. Because these small upsets occur so regularly, they end up affecting us the most.

Daily causes of stress include:

• **Environmental stressors** – Your physical surroundings can set off the stress response. Examples of environmental stressors include an unsafe neighborhood, pollution, noise (sirens keeping you up at night, a barking dog next door), and uncomfortable living conditions. For people living in crime-ridden areas or war-torn regions, the stress may be unrelenting.

• **Family and relationship stressors** – Problems with friends, romantic partners, and family members are common daily stressors. Marital disagreements, dysfunctional relationships, rebellious teens, or caring for a chronically-ill family member or a child with special needs can all send stress levels skyrocketing.

• **Work stressors** – In our career-driven society, work can be an ever-present source of stress. Work stress is caused by things such as job dissatisfaction, an exhausting workload, insufficient pay, office politics, and conflicts with your boss or co-workers.

• **Social stressors** – Your social situation can cause stress. For example, poverty, financial pressures, racial and sexual discrimination or harassment, unemployment, isolation, and a lack of social support all take a toll on daily quality of life.

**Types of Stress and Health Hazards**

According to American Psychological Association (APA), there are 3 different types stress — acute stress, episodic acute stress, and chronic stress. The 3 types of stress each have their own characteristics, symptoms, duration, and treatment approaches.

Stress management can be complicated because each of the 3 different types of stress can present as single, repeated, complicated, or chronic. Therefore, they require different levels of treatment interventions, management, and psychological treatment modalities due to the nature of the person's environment, lifestyle, developmental history, coping resources, and personality.

**ACUTE STRESS**

Acute stress is usually brief. It is the most common and frequent presentation. Acute stress is most often caused by reactive thinking. Negative thoughts predominate about situations or events that have recently occurred, or upcoming situations, events, or demands in the near future.

For example, if you have recently been involved in an argument, you may have acute stress related to negative thoughts that are repetitive about the argument. Or you may have acute stress that is about an upcoming work deadline, again the stress is thought induced. However, most often when the thinking-induced stress is reduced or removed the stress will subside too. However, if the stress meets DSM-5 criteria, then individual may be diagnosed with Acute Stress Disorder

Acute stress causes signs and symptoms in the body + brain + emotions, but does not cause the significant amount of damage as Episodic Stress and Chronic stress.

**Short-term Effects of Acute Stress**

The most common signs + symptoms:

- Transient Emotional distress — some combination of anger or irritability, anxiety and depression.

- Transient Muscular distress—tension, headache, back pain, neck pain, jaw pain, and other muscular tensions that lead to pulled muscles and tendons and ligament problems.

- Transient stomach, gut and bowel problems, heartburn, acid stomach, flatulence, diarrhea, constipation.

- Transient hyperarousal—elevated blood pressure, rapid heartbeat, rapid pulse, sweaty palms, heart palpitations, dizziness, migraine headaches, cold hands or feet, shortness of breath, sleep problems, and chest pain.

Acute stress can present in anyone's life. It is highly treatable and manageable.

However, repeated acute stress can become very harmful for your physical and mental health.

**Episodic Acute Stress**

People who frequently experience acute stress, or whose lives present with frequent triggers of stress, have episodic acute stress.

The individuals who frequently suffer acute stress often live a life of chaos and crisis. They are always in a rush or feel pressured. They take on many responsibilities, and usually cannot stay organized with so many time demands. These individuals are perpetually in the grips of acute stress overload.

**There are 2 main personality types that frequently present with Episodic Acute Stress:**

1) "Type A" personality

2) The "Worrier"

**"Type A" personality**: Type A personality have an excessive competitive drive, aggressiveness, impatience, abrupt, and a sense of time urgency. In addition, Type A personality presents as reactive with hostility, and almost always a deep-seated insecurity about performance. These personality traits create frequent episodes of acute stress for the Type A individual. The cardiologists, Friedman and Rosenman found Type A's to be significantly likely to develop coronary heart disease.

**The "Worrier"**: The Worrier presents with almost incessant negative thoughts causing episodic acute stress on physical and mental health. "Worry warts" project probable disaster and negatively forecast catastrophe in almost every situation. They have core beliefs that the world is a dangerous, unrewarding, punitive place where something awful is always about to happen. These negative binge thinkers also tend to be over aroused and tense, but are more anxious and depressed than angry and hostile. Their thoughts are frequently filled with "What if...." statements that are with projected negative outcomes. They are often diagnosed DSM-5 with generalized anxiety disorder.

**Episodic Effects of Acute Stress**

The most common signs + symptoms are similar to acute stress, but due to the extended frequent over arousal or extended hyperarousal there is ongoing damage and suffering.

- Emotional distress —anger or irritability, anxiety and depression, short-tempered, impatient, tense.
- Cognitive distress: compromised attention/concentration, compromised processing speed, compromised new learning and new learning memory consolidation and retrieval, and mental fatigue.
- Interpersonal relationships deteriorate the workplace becomes a very stressful place for them.
- Muscular distress—tension, headache, back pain, jaw pain, pulled muscles, tendons, and ligament problems.
- Stomach, gut, bowel problems, heartburn, acid stomach, flatulence, diarrhea, constipation, irritable bowel syndrome (IBS).
- High blood pressure, rapid heartbeat, sweaty palms, heart palpitations, dizziness, migraine headaches, cold hands or feet, shortness of breath, insomnia, chest pain, and heart disease.
- Immune System Compromise: frequent colds/flu, allergies, asthma, and other immune system compromise illnesses.

Episodic acute stress leads to more pronounced health issues such as, high blood pressure and heart disease, and irritable bowel syndrome (IBS).

**CHRONIC STRESS**

Chronic stress is the most harmful type of stress. If chronic stress is left untreated over a long period of time, it can significantly and often irreversibly damage your physical health and deteriorate your mental health.

For example, long term poverty, repeated abuse in any form, unemployment, dysfunctional family, poor work environment, substance abuse, or an unhappy marriage can cause significant chronic stress.

Chronic stress can also set in when an individual feels hopeless, does not see an escape from the cause of stress, and gives up on seeking solutions.

Chronic stress can be caused by aversive experiences in childhood or traumatic experiences later in life.

When an individual lives with chronic stress, his/her behavioral actions and emotional reactions become ingrained. There is change in the hardwiring of the neurobiology of the brain and body. There by making them constantly prone to the hazardous stress effects on the body + mind+ cognitive regardless of the scenarios.

People with chronic stress have the list of signs and symptoms previously mentioned, but the signs and symptoms are chronic and can result in a physical and mental breakdown that can lead to suicide, violent actions, homicide, psychosis, heart attacks, and strokes.

Chronic stress is grinding stress. It wears people away day after day, year after year. Chronic stress destroys lives, bodies, and minds. It wreaks havoc through long-term attrition. It is the stress of poverty, dysfunctional families, violence, abuse, trauma, despised job, ethnic rivalry, war.

**Stages of Stress (It's Important to Know Which One You're In)**

**Stage 1: Fight or Flight**

The moment you first feel stressed, your body lets you know. It sounds the alarm and activity in the thyroid and adrenal glands is increased. This is what happens when you hear about entrepreneurs "burning out." Their adrenal glands go into overload because the fire alarm is going off, and yet they're still sitting there in their office working.

When you don't pay attention to these alarms, other things within your body start happening. There is an increase in stress hormones, heart rate, blood pressure, and even a decrease in short-term memory and feelings of stress, fear, anxiety and depression.

Now, the flip-side to all this is that in the alarm stage, your mental focus also tends to increase. Not for long, but initially.

**Stage 2: Damage Control**

When your body feels stressed, it knows it.

What happens, then, is it does its best to keep things as normal as possible while your body works overtime. Anti-inflammatory hormones (cortisol) are secreted in order to control the inflammation that's happening. But this is not a long-term solution. It's a quick fix to keep things moving while issues are sorted out.

Again, entrepreneurs are notorious for knowing these alarms are going off but pushing through regardless. In fact, we praise the behavior.

**Stage 3: Recovery**

At some point, hopefully you've acknowledged that you've been running a marathon at a sprint pace and decided it's time to take a step back.

When you begin recovery, your body does its best to return your internal systems to their original and healthy levels.

In order to recover, though, you have to rest, sleep, and reduce overall output--something that's incredibly difficult for entrepreneurs.

**Stage 4: Adaption**

Now, let's say you didn't listen to your body and you decided not to make time to recover.

You've chosen to "adapt" instead.

Essentially, what you're telling your body is that this level of stress isn't going to go away anytime soon. So, what does it do? It begins to settle into the feeling of constant stress, and adapts accordingly.

Except, that doesn't necessarily mean it adapts in a good way.

What you'll start to feel then is everything from lower energy levels to a demolished self-esteem. You won't sleep as well, you might gain (or lose) unhealthy amounts of weight, and be far less likely to manage your emotions.

**Stage 5: Burnout**

And finally, should you ignore the first four stages of warning, you will eventually find yourself completely and utterly "burned out."

This could mean everything from full-fledged depression to actually being hospitalized.

It's amazing that in the entrepreneurship community, things such as lack of sleep and non-stop grinding are celebrated as accolades that prove your devotion to the journey. I, myself, talk a lot about the work required in order to be successful. But I also know that if it isn't kept in balance, then the short-term gain will end up becoming a loss in the long run.

You are your most important asset. If you don't keep yourself balanced, you will suffer (mentally, physically, emotionally).

**Managing stress**

Without a proper support system in place, people often turn to unhealthy techniques to manage their stress, particularly Millennials with high money stress. For example, of all Americans, 38% say they surf the internet to manage stress, while 67% of Millennials say the same. For eating to deal with stress, the breakdown is 23% to 41%, respectively. Alcohol use for stress management is nearly double at 12% for all Americans and 25% for Millennials.

However, when emotional support is available (family, friends, or professional help such as an employee assistance program) we see significant improvement in overall stress:

- 43% of respondents without emotional support say stress has increased in the past year

- 26% of respondents with emotional support say stress has increased in the past year

Those with emotional support are able to handle stress and its effects better than those without:

- 46% of people without emotional support felt depressed due to stress in the last month
- 32% of people with emotional support felt depressed due to stress in the last month.

The overall positive effects of an emotional support system are extremely encouraging. When individuals can turn to trained professionals with their stress problems, they are less likely to engage in unhealthy behavior, and are more likely to be productive at work, and maintain healthier relationships. A professional assistance program can offer a wide variety of trainings, counseling services, and referrals to help people learn how to effectively manage their stress.

# CHAPTER TWO

# Stress Management Concept, Facts, Tips, Techniques And Strategies

**Introduction**

What happens when we continue "burning the candle at both ends" until we reach physical and emotional exhaustion? Just like the candle itself, we risk burning ourselves out. There is a parable of a frog sitting in a pot on the stove. If dropped into a pot of boiling water, a frog would likely notice and try to escape. But when placed in a pot that is slowly approaching a boil, the frog doesn't notice until the water has already reached an unbearable heat—at which point it is too hot for the frog to survive. Have you ever experienced a slow acceptance of the pressures around you, until everything is "just too much" and you can barely cope? If so, you're not alone. About 8.3 million American adults were reported to have experienced serious psychological distress in 2017 ("More Americans suffering from stress, anxiety, and depression, study finds," 2018). *So what if we could notice the boiling signs earlier and even "turns down" the heat?* If stress "has become one of the most serious health issues of the 20th century and a worldwide epidemic," then it is time to start growing our tools in handling stress ("Workplace Stress," 2018).Present chapter on Stress Management Concept, Facts, Tips, Techniques and Strategies.

## *Concept of Stress Management*

Stress is basically the tension or anxiety caused by any sort of pressure in everyday life. The ability to handle or minimize the physical and emotional effects of such anxiety is known as one's stress management skills. The importance given to stress management skills in workplace can be guessed from the fact that employers, in many countries, have been burdened with a legal responsibility of recognizing as well as coping with the workplace stress in order to ensure good mental and physical health of employees in organization. Put simply, stress management is:

*"Set of techniques and programs intended to help people deal more effectively with stress in their lives by analyzing the specific stressors and taking positive actions to minimize their effects"*

*-Gale Encyclopedia of Medicine, 2008*

Popular examples of stress management include meditation, yoga, and exercise. We'll explore these in detail, with a range of different approaches to ensure that there's something that works for everyone. First, let's set one thing straight: we're not aiming towards being stress-free all of the time. That's unrealistic. After all, it's an unavoidable human response that we all experience from time to time—and it's not all bad either. However, we can all benefit from identifying our stress and managing it better.

*Stress is the "psychological, physiological and behavioral response by an individual when they perceive a lack of equilibrium between the demands placed upon them and their ability to meet those demands, which, over a period of time, leads to ill-health"*

*-Palmer, 1989*

**Symptoms of stress**

Although we all experience stress differently, some common symptoms include:

- Difficulty concentrating
- Difficulty sleeping
- Excessive sleeping
- Fatigue
- Feeling overwhelmed
- Headaches
- Heartburn
- Irritability
- Nausea
- Obsessive or compulsive behaviors
- Panic attacks
- Social isolation

- Stomach pain
- Sweaty hands or feet
- Teeth grinding
- Weight gain or weight loss

**Stress helpful and harmful**

Historically, stress was our friend. It acted as a protective mechanism that warned us of danger; a natural reaction that told us when to run. This response is now referred to as the "fight or flight" response, or the "stress response." When your evolutionary ancestors saw a saber-toothed cat and ran from it, stress saved their life. Stress has remained part of the evolutionary drive because of its usefulness in survival. When used at the right time, stress increases our awareness and improves physical performance in short bursts (Van Duyne, 2003).Repetitive exposure of the stress response on our body is proven to lead to long-lasting psychological and physical health issues; these include cardiovascular disease, diabetes, anxiety and depression ("How Does Stress Affect Us?" 2016).

**Stress versus burnout**

What's the difference between stress and burnout? Stress is inevitable. Burnout isn't. While stress is our response, burnout is the accumulation of excessive stressors over time, which results in unmanageable stress levels. American psychologist Herbert Freudenberg first termed the word "burnout" in the 1970s, referring to the effect of extreme stress and high ideals placed on "helping" professionals, such as doctors and nurses ("Depression: What is burnout?", 2018). Today, the word has evolved. It is now used more broadly to refer to the consequences of "excessive stress" placed on any individual, no matter their occupation. When we get to the point of no longer being able to cope, we are "burned out," like a candle. This is where stress management can offer tools, and help people avoid the unpleasant experience of burnout.

**Facts about Stress & Burnout**

If you're not yet convinced about the need to prioritize stress management, these facts might help:

- Chronic stress can place pressure on, and cause damage to arteries and organs. This occurs due to inflation in our bodies caused by cytokines (a result of stress) (McEwen, 2003).

- Correlations have been found between stress and the top six causes of death: cancer, lung ailments, heart disease, liver cirrhosis, accidents, and suicide ("How Does Stress Affect Us?", 2016).
- In children, chronic stress has been found to negatively impact their developmental growth due to a reduction of the growth hormone in the pituitary gland (Van der Kolk, B. et. al., 2007).
- In the event of chronic stress, dominant hormones are released into our brain. These hormones are intended for short-term emergencies and in the event where they exist for extended periods they can shrink, impair and kill brain cells (Wallenstein, 2003).
- More good news, especially for chocolate lovers—dark chocolate has been found to reduce stress hormones (Wallenstein, 2003).
- On a positive note, we can reduce our stress levels by laughing. Having a chuckle, lowers the stress hormones, including cortical, epinephrine, and adrenaline. Laughing also strengthens our immune system by releasing positive hormones (Wallenstein, 2003).
- Researchers have found that stress worsens acne, more so than the prevalence of oily skin (Warner, 2002).
- Stress accounts for 30% of all infertility problems. In women, stress can cause spasms in the fallopian tubes and uterus. In men, it can reduce sperm count and cause erectile dysfunction (Bouchez, 2018).
- Stress can cause weight gain too. The stress hormone cortisol has been found to cause both the accumulation of abdominal fat and the enlargement of fat cells, causing "diseased" fat (Chilnick, 2008).
- Stress can increase the likelihood of developing blood clots since the blood prepares itself for injuries and becomes "stickier" (Chilnick, 2008).
- Stress has been referred to as the "silent killer" as it can cause heart disease, high blood pressure, chest pain, and an irregular heartbeat (Chilnick, 2008).
- Stress is also responsible for altering our blood sugar levels, which can lead to fatigue, hyperglycemia, mood swings, and metabolic syndrome ("How Does Stress Affect Us?", 2016).
- Telogen effluvium is the result of hair loss caused by stress that can happen up to three months after a stressful event (McEwen, 2003).
- The word itself, "stress" stems from the Latin word stringere, meaning "to draw tight" (McEwen, 2003).

**Tips for Stress Management**

Before discussing stress management techniques, there are several factors to consider. The following tips are adapted from The American Psychological Association ("Check out the Stress Tip Sheet," 2018) to support individuals with a stress management plan:

- Ask for support when needed. If you're feeling overwhelmed, reach out to a friend or family member you can talk to. Speaking with a healthcare professional can also reduce stress, and help us learn healthier coping strategies.
- Identify your stress sources. What causes you to be stressed? Be it work, family, change or any of the other potential thousand triggers.
- Implement healthy stress management strategies. It's good to be mindful of any current unhealthy coping behaviors so you can switch them out for a healthy option. For example, if overeating is your current go to, you could practice meditation instead, or make a decision to phone a friend to chat through your situation. The American Psychological Association suggests that switching out one behavior at a time is most effective in creating positive change.
- Learn to recognize stress signals. We all process stress differently so it's important to be aware of your individual stress symptoms. What are your internal alarm bells? Low tolerance, headaches, stomach pains or a combination from the above 'Symptoms of stress'
- Make self-care a priority. When we make time for ourselves, we put our well-being before others. This can feel selfish to start, but it is like the airplane analogy—we must put our own oxygen mask on before we can assist others. The simplest things that promote well-being, such as enough sleep, food, downtime, and exercise are often the ones overlooked.
- Recognize your stress strategies. What is your go-to tactic for calming down? These can be behaviors learned over years and sometimes aren't the healthy option. For example, some people cope with stress by self-medicating with alcohol or overeating.
- Understand your stress. How do you stress? It can be different for everybody. By understanding what stress looks like for you, you can be better prepared, and reach for your stress management toolbox when needed.

**Different Stress Management Techniques & Strategies**

These tips are thing we can all benefit from doing more of. The techniques are categorized into three groups:

1. Action Orientated Approaches: used to take action to change a stressful situation
2. Emotion-oriented approaches: used to change the way we perceive a stressful situation
3. Acceptance-oriented approaches: used for dealing with stressful situations you can't control

Explore the below options and find what combination works best for keeping your stress levels under control.

Action-Orientated Approaches. Action-oriented approaches allow you to take action and change the stressful situation. As Nelson & Hurrell said: *"Stress is inevitable, distress is not"*

- **ABC Technique.** The ABC technique was also originally created by psychologist Dr. Albert Ellis and was later adapted by Martin Seligman. The letters ABC stand for; A – adversity, or the stressful event. B – Beliefs, or the way that you respond to the event. Then C – consequences, the result of your beliefs lead to the actions and outcome of that event. Essentially, the more optimistic your beliefs, the more positive the outcome.

**Acceptance-Orientated Approaches.** Acceptance-oriented approaches are useful in stressful situations that you cannot control. Epictetus, the Greek philosopher had it right when he said: *"Men are disturbed not by things but by the views they take of them"*

- Affirmations and imagery. The power of positive imagery and affirmations is now scientifically proven to increase positive emotion. How? When you think of a positive experience, your brain perceives it to be a reality. So, replace those negative thoughts with positive statements and challenge and change the way you see and experience the world.
- Be assertive. Clear and effective communication is the key to being assertive. When we're assertive, we can ask for what we want or need,

and also explain what is bothering us. The key is doing this in a fair and firm manner while still having empathy for others. Once you identify what you need to communicate, you can stand up for yourself and be proactive in altering the stressful situation.

- Build resilience. Resiliency is our ability to bounce back from stressful or negative experiences. To simplify, resilient people are skilled at accepting that the situation has occurred, they learn from what transpired and then they move on.

- Cognitive Restructuring. In the mid-1950's psychologist Dr. Albert Ellis developed what cognitive restructuring, a technique for understanding negative emotions and challenging the sometimes incorrect beliefs that cause them. Cognitive restructuring is a key component of Cognitive behavioral therapy (CBT).

- Creating boundaries. Boundaries are the internal set of rules that we establish for ourselves. They outline what behaviors we will and won't accept, how much time and space we need from others, and what priorities we have. *Healthy boundaries are essential for a stress-free life. When we have healthy boundaries we respect ourselves and take care of our well-being by clearly expressing our boundaries to others.* Watch this video to help establish healthy boundaries: One of the tips in the video can help you prioritize your wants. For example, let's say you are invited to a social event this weekend, but you have not had any time for yourself. The idea of reading a book and eating Chinese take-out sounds like your dream, but you're afraid of hurting someone's feelings if you don't attend. It could be helpful to consider what you would do, if no one cared either way. If no one cares, maybe you decide to have a low-key evening by yourself. If someone really cares, and that relationship matters to you, you'd probably benefit more from making an appearance at the event.

- Diet and Exercise. You've heard it before, but you are what you eat. Be mindful of having a balanced and healthy diet. Making simple diet changes, such as reducing your alcohol, caffeine and sugar intake is a proven way of reducing anxiety. Another guaranteed way to reduce stress is exercise. It's proven to also be as effective as antidepressants in relieving mild depression. *So... get moving! (We know it's easier said than done).*

- Get out of your head. Sometimes it's best not to even try contending with the racing thoughts. Sometimes you just need a break. Distract yourself. Watch a movie, phone or catch up with a friend, go for a walk, or do something positive that you know takes your mind off things.

**Emotion–Orientated Approaches.** Emotion-oriented approaches are used to change the way we perceive stressful situations. In the words of William James: *"The greatest weapon against stress is our ability to choose one thought over another"*

- Manage your time. If we let them, our days will consume us. Before we know it, the months have become overwhelmingly busy. When we prioritize and organize our tasks, we create a less stressful and more enjoyable life.
- Meditation and physical relaxation. Use techniques such as deep breathing, guided visualizations, yoga, and guided body scans. These activities help relax the body. Some examples for you to try out are included below.
- Reduce the noise. Switching off all the technology, screen time, and constant stimuli can help us slow down. How often do you go offline? It is worth changing, for your own sake. Make time for some quietness each day. You may notice how all those seemingly urgent things we need to do become less important and crisis-like. That to-do list will be there when you're in a place to return to it. Remember that recharging is a very effective way of tackling stress.
- Sleep. Getting a good night sleep is fundamental for recharging and dealing with stressful situations in the best possible way. While it varies from individual to individual, on the exact amount of sleep needed, an uninterrupted sleep of approximately 8 hours is generally recommended.
- Talk it out. Don't hold it all inside. Talk to someone close to you about your worries or the things getting you down. Sharing worries can cut them in half, and also give you a chance to laugh at potentially absurd situations. *Many of our worries sound a lot less worrisome when we say them out loud.* If you don't feel up to sharing, writing them down is also a great way to release them. Or maybe engage with an independent professional.

**Importance of Stress management**

A certain level of stress is always present in any workplace. As soon as the level of stress escalates to a point that it becomes dangerous for the well-being of the organization as well as employees, stress management becomes important. It has the following benefits:

- Enables you to motivate employees better. Stressful situation can have a devastating effect on the morale of employees, causing increased absenteeism and employee turnover. However, good stress management skills help the morale of employees to stay intact so that they are more motivated and better focused on their jobs and performance.
- For a better life. Learning stress management skills and applying them to everyday life helps a person take control of his or her life. Handling stress effectively builds a positive outlook. A solution-oriented approach helps in overcoming problems and living a better life. Having a purpose also helps you find your way through challenging and stressful situations. Your sense of purpose provides a strong foundation that enables you to climb out of difficult situations.
- Improves productivity even in stressful situations. Since the employee morale and workplace relationships remain intact, stress management skills are considered to be one of the major contributors to the improved productivity. With ideal stress management skills, there will be lesser chances of customer complaints or poor decision-making even in the most stressful circumstances.
- Reduced chances of workplace conflicts. Among many other factors contributing to workplace conflicts such as differences in opinions, backgrounds and personalities, the increased level of stress also plays a major role. It shatters the workplace relationships, undermining the overall culture. However, effective stress management skills prevent such distractions and builds teamwork, making everyone's lives easier and fun.
- To enhance performance. Stress at work has become common in today's fast-paced world. Workplace stress hampers one's ability to perform well and succeed. Workplace stress may lead to emotional burnout, low self-esteem, or a feeling of worthlessness. It can also impact your career growth. Hence, believe in the importance of stress management in an organization and take necessary steps to reduce stress. Don't be stressed about things that are beyond your control.
- To improve communication. Once you start handling stress, everything falls in place. Stress management starts untangling your problems. Your communication process improves. You open up more and try to express

your feelings. Misunderstandings are cleared.

- To improve health. Constantly being under stress affects your health. It makes you prone to various diseases and accelerates your aging process. Research shows that stressed individuals age faster than those who are stress-free. Stress also causes weight gain and obesity. It is important to identify and treat stress at an early stage in order to lead a healthy life.
- To move on. Jim Carrey, a famous actor, has acknowledged that he had suffered from stress and depression. He describes how he felt it was necessary to get out of bed every day and say that life is good. Though it was difficult for him at times, he did this. So it's imperative to sort things out and move on. Eating healthy was one of his tools to battle stress.
- To strengthen relationships. It takes no time for relationships to collapse under stress. Building or re-building trust and bridging the communication gap are the right things to do. If you value your relationships and want them to survive the storm, opt for suitable stress management techniques.

**Improve stress management skills**

Bearing in mind how too much stress can be detrimental to employees' morale and organization's profits level, following measures can be taken to improve stress management skills:

- Identify the sources of stress and prioritize. There can be personal as well as workplace pressures causing stress. The first step towards improvement of stress management skills is to be able to identify the source causing it. Once identified, make a priority list and tackle the stressors one at a time. Being more organized sometimes helps in relieving part of the stress.
- Manage stress through exercise. Take care of your physical health by eating healthy, avoiding excessive sugar and, most of all, exercising regularly. Learn yoga as well as other exercises for muscle relaxation. This will help you manage your physical responses to a stressful situation.
- Motivate yourself to find solutions. There are many ways you can boost up your morale for managing stress. For example, make a list of similar situations you have managed to handle in the past and recall how you did it, or promise yourself a reward after you have successfully managed to cope with the stressful situation. However, if the stressors are things that

are completely out of your control, you must be able to remind yourself and be okay with the fact that there is nothing you can do.

## Conclusion

What happens when we continue "burning the candle at both ends" until we reach physical and emotional exhaustion? Just like the candle itself, we risk burning ourselves out. There is a parable of a frog sitting in a pot on the stove. If dropped into a pot of boiling water, a frog would likely notice and try to escape. But when placed in a pot that is slowly approaching a boil, the frog doesn't notice until the water has already reached an unbearable heat—at which point it is too hot for the frog to survive. Have you ever experienced a slow acceptance of the pressures around you, until everything is "just too much" and you can barely cope? If so, you're not alone. About 8.3 million American adults were reported to have experienced serious psychological distress in 2017 ("More Americans suffering from stress, anxiety, and depression, study finds," 2018). *So what if we could notice the boiling signs earlier and even "turns down" the heat?* If stress "has become one of the most serious health issues of the 20th century and a worldwide epidemic," then it is time to start growing our tools in handling stress ("Workplace Stress," 2018).Present chapter on Stress Management Concept, Facts, Tips, Techniques and Strategies. Put simply, stress management is: *"Set of techniques and programs intended to help people deal more effectively with stress in their lives by analyzing the specific stressors and taking positive actions to minimize their effects"-Gale Encyclopedia of Medicine, 2008.* Although we all experience stress differently, some common symptoms include: Difficulty concentrating, Difficulty sleeping, Excessive sleeping, Fatigue, Feeling overwhelmed, Headaches, Heartburn, Irritability, Nausea, Obsessive or compulsive behaviors, Panic attacks, Social isolation, Stomach pain, Sweaty hands or feet, Teeth grinding and Weight gain or weight loss. The American Psychological Association ("Check out the Stress Tip Sheet," 2018) to support individuals with a stress management plan as Ask for support when needed, Identify your stress sources, Implement healthy stress management strategies, Learn to recognize stress signals, Make self-care a priority. When we make time for ourselves, we put our well-being before others. This can feel selfish to start, but it is like the airplane analogy—we must put our own oxygen mask on before we can assist others, Recognize your stress strategies and Understand your stress. The techniques are categorized into three groups as Action Orientated Approaches: used to take action to change a stressful situation, Emotion-oriented approaches: used to change the way we perceive a stressful situation and Acceptance-oriented approaches: used for dealing with stressful situations you can't control. Importance of Stress management as Enables you to motivate employees better, For a better life, Improves productivity even in stressful situations, Reduced chances of workplace conflicts, To enhance performance, To improve communication, To improve health, To move on and To strengthen relationships. Improve stress management skills as identify the sources of stress and prioritize, Manage stress through exercise and motivate you to find solutions.

# CHAPTER THREE

# Causes of Stress and Stress Management among Students at Home and at School or College, A Comparative Study

## Introduction

It is very difficult to find a proper definition of 'Stress'. Psychologists gave different concepts of "Stress" in different ways. According to Hans Selye (1950) stress is "The non-specific response of the body to any demand."

Lazarus and Folkman (1984) defined stress as" A pattern of negative physiological responses occurring in situations where people perceive threats to their well-being which they may be unable to meet".

Roz Brody, R and D Dwyer (2002) also defined stress as" A state of physiological and physical tension produced, according to the transactional model, when there is a mismatch between the perceived demands of a situation (the stressor) and the individual's perceived ability to cope. The consequent state of tension can be adaptive or maladaptive".

So basically from all these statements, we can summarise that Stress is a negative feeling created by the outside environment or stimulus which comes from over demand of the work or society which is higher than the ability of an individual(person).

It is a common problem in modern days and there is no way to escape it. Stress becomes both helpful or harmful for us. It helps us to motivate and do the work under deadlines or perform work under pressure which builds up our working strength. But on the other hand it can cause anxiety, depression, restlessness, lack of motivation and many more.

Now a days, work pressure on the work place becomes a common event where employees have high targets, projects pressure, client pressure, incremental pressure etc. But there are another large section of the society who are not exempted from the circle of stress and these are the students. Not only at the school but also they are pressurised at their home. Where as the school students face the stress from parents, tuition, study and peer pressure, financial expenses and over-commitment. The college students face the stress from job findings, marriage, family expectations, project deadlines etc.

A mild amount of stress is very useful and acts as a motivation for students but too much stress can interfere with their daily lives.

Stress can cause many serious problems like depression and anxiety. Managing stress from early ages can help to enhance the college/university experience and opportunities for students.

**Stressor:**

The stress causing factors are known as Stressor. It includes physical, mental, emotional or cultural factors like financial crisis, parent's behaviouretc.

**Types of Stress:**

There are three types of stress based on exposure of stress-causing factors. These are –

1. Acute Stress: It is the most common type of stress. It is created by recent or unexpected events or challenges. This is also known as present stress. Sometimes it may be severe if someone experiences some crime scene or accident.

2. Episodic Acute Stress: If someone frequently exposes to the chains of events causes acute stress, it is known as episodic acute stress. It creates behavioural problems in the individual and destroys all the relationships the person has.

3. Chronic Stress: This stress is created by long term problems like financial problems, family problems, marriage problems etc. Most of the adult faces this type of stress.It also harms someone's physical health. Only doctor can help someone to fight against this stress.

Beside that on the basis of impact of stress on body, mind and performance, stress can be categorized into two types. These are-

1. Eu-stress- It is the optimal amount of stress that a person can handle. This stress is helpful for us. It teaches a person how to manage time and also helps to motivate themselves. It also helps an individual to find his hidden talent.

2. Distress- It is the excessive amount of stress that is not controllable. This stress is harmful to anyone. Distress can cause harmful effects on body, mind and activities.Some effects include depression, heart attack etc.

**How to detect a person having stress?**

A person with stress shows some physical, psychological and behavioural symptoms by which we can easily identify them. These symptoms are-

**1. Physical symptoms:**
•Headache
•Muscular tension
•Fatigue
•Insomnia or sleeping problems
•Faster heart beat

**2.Psychological symptoms :**
•Depression
•Anxiety
•Unable to cope with any situation
•Lack of concentration
•Unable to make decisions

**3. Behavioural symptoms:**
•Absent from the school/College / Workplace.
•Drop in performance
•Mood swing
•Impatience and frustration
•Lack of interest in any work
•Problems in relationship
•Isolation

In this article we are discussing about the stress causing factors(which affect students the most) and the stress management procedures (taken by themselves to relief the stress) provided by the students of different standard(High school, pursuing Graduation, pursuing post graduation ).

**Research Sample:**

Here a sample of total 150 students from different classes and streams( 50 students from each category like Class 11-12, Pursuing Graduation, Pursuing Post Graduation from different schools and institutes of Agartala, Tripura) were collected to make a comparative study.

**Procedure:**

- Prepare a questionnaire
- Create an online link
- Collect the answers from different students. ( 50 students from each category like Class 11-12, Pursuing Graduation, Pursuing Post Graduation).
- Results put on graph or chart to make a comparative study.

**Observation:**

Here in this study we collected two types of observations

A.About the most common stress stimulating factor among students (one student gave more than one reason of stresses)

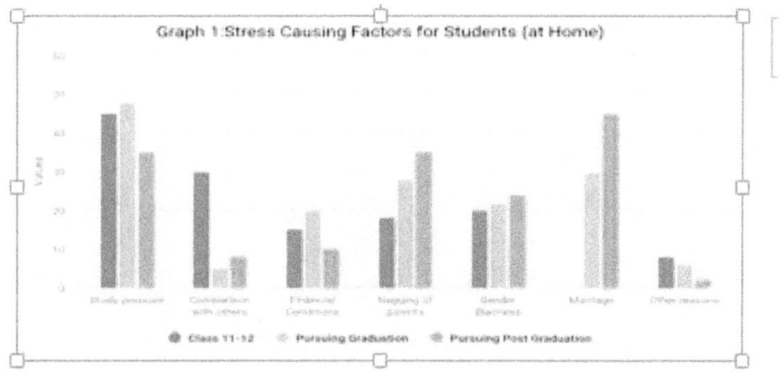

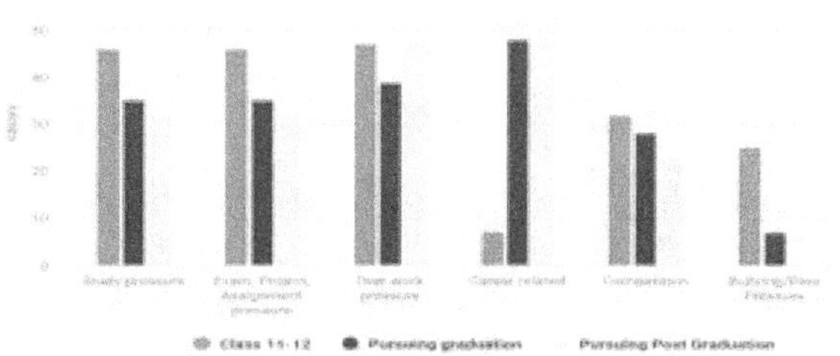

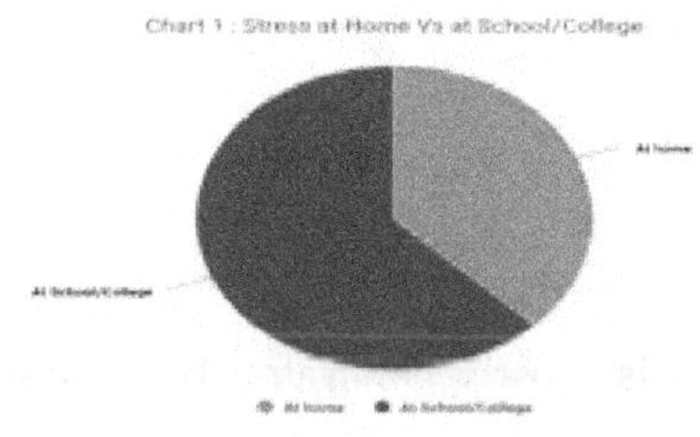

B. The methods the students use to get rid off from the stress.
(One student answered more than one method of stress management )

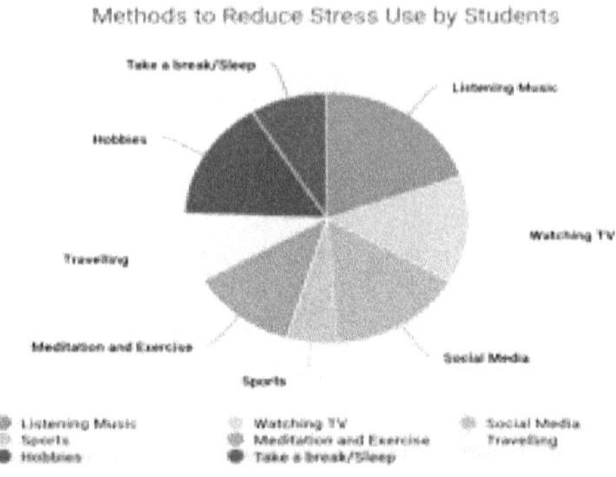



**Result:**

In this study, three types of students(class 11-12, pursuing Graduation and pursuing Post Graduation were considered who are belong to the age group of 15 to 30years. Surprisingly it is found that one factor if considered as stress factor for certain classes, is no longer stress factor for other classes. The problems of Graduation and Post graduation students are similar in nature.

**A)The common stress factors are-**

**At Home:**

•Study pressure: This stress is mostly generated by parents. They always want that their children get high rank or good marks in the examination without knowing their performance ability.

•Nagging of parents: After adolescence students are able to think about themselves. But parent's "do's and don't list" always pressurise them.

•Comparison with others/siblings: "Look at them, dress like them, study like them, why don't you get marks like them?" these words of comparison are common stress enhancers among students.

•Personal circumstances: Quarrels between parents, domestic violence also causes stress among them.

•Financial Conditions: Problems in financial condition also damages mental health.

•Health issues/Disability: Disabled people are categorized as marginalized. These behaviour from others make them stressed.

•Gender biasness: Mainly girl child faces this situation at home.

•Pressure for marriage: After Graduation, parents force them for marry which creates stress on them.

**At School/College:**

•Study pressure: Academic pressure put by the teachers and professors causes study pressure.

•Exam, Assignment, Project Pressure: Semester system, and project loads are others reasons of stress.

• Overwork pressure: Overwork pressure causes distress and harm one's physical and mental health.

•Bullying/Peer pressure: Weak students are always the victims of the stronger ones and it is the reason of stress among them.

•Competition: The imbalance between performance and demand or simply fear of lose in competition causes stress.

•Finding job/Career oriented: Nowadays it is not easy to find proper job with respect to your qualification and this is another reason of stress in educated people.

Most of the teenagers said that the stress was created mostly by their school. The study, exam pressures were sometimes intolerable for them. A very few said about the stress from financial crisis and comparison with others.

On the other hand, the students pursuing Graduation and Post Graduation were mostly affected by their home. Pressure for marriage, quitting their study, and finding job were the common reasons of stress for them.

**B)The students also use some methods to reduce their stress levels.**

These are-

•Listening to music: Good and relaxing music slower the heart rate and blood pressure and reduce the levels of stress hormones.

•Watching television, and Web series: Some entertainment is also good for stress relief.

•Social media: Spending time on social media is good for stress regulation.

•Sports: Sports help to gain the confidence that someone lose due to stress.

•Meditation and Exercise: Both of them release good hormones in body which can help to feel less stressed.

•Get more involved into hobbies: Hobbies like painting, dancing, singing fresh our mood and reduce the stress.

•Reading novels : Break from curriculum or text book and reading an interesting novel or story reduces stress.

•Conversation with others/Gossiping: Talking to friends and closed one helps to find out the solution of stressor and helps to relieve the stress.

•Travelling: Travelling can take out someone from their daily schedule. It is also making someone feel calm

•Take a break/Proper sleep: Take a break for some time from all works and proper sleep also helps to relieve stress.

Stress management methods are common among all the classes, but the most used one is listening the music.

**Conclusion:**

Stress is the factor which is knowingly or unknowingly hamper our life and we cannot get rid off it unless we overcome it..Managing stress in different ways helps to reduce the stress. We have to remember, no one is Perfect, we are not robots and over workload can only damage our health. So, it is our responsibility that we should not underestimate ourselves. Truthful thinking, proper practises, effortless manner, positive attitude only helps us to manage our stress because ***ADAPTABILITY IS THE MOTHER KEY TO CONVERT DISTRESS TO EUSTRESS.***

# CHAPTER FOUR

# Motivation: A Tool To Overcome Stress

## Introduction

Stress is a natural human response that occurs to everyone. The human body is, in reality, built to feel stress and react to it. Your body creates physical and mental responses when you encounter changes or problems (stressors). Stress is that. Stress reactions help the body adapt to new circumstances. Stress can be optimistic, keeping us alert, encouraged and prepared to prevent risk. To some extent, everyone feels tension. However, the way you respond to stress makes a huge difference to your overall well-being. The best way to handle your stress often includes adjusting your situation. At other times, the best solution includes adjusting the way you react to the situation. It is not always easy to recognize stress, but there are some ways to recognise some indicators that too much pressure might be encountered. Stress can often come from an obvious place, but even tiny everyday stresses from work, school, family, and friends can sometimes damage your mind and body. The autonomic nervous system of the body regulates your heart rate, breathing, changes in your vision, and more. The "fight-or-flight response," its built-in stress reaction, helps the body face stressful conditions. Continued activation of the stress response causes wear and tear on the body when a person has long-term (chronic) stress. They experience physical, emotional and behavioral symptoms.

Stress management is a broad spectrum of strategies and psychotherapies to regulate the level of stress of an individual, particularly chronic stress, typically for the purpose of improving daily functioning and for purpose of improving it. Stress causes various physical and mental symptoms that differ according to the situational variables of each person. This may involve deteriorating physical health as well as depression. The stress management method is known as one of the keys in modern society to a stable and healthy life. While life poses various requirements that can be difficult to cope with, stress management offers a variety of ways to control anxiety and maintain overall well-being.

## 1. Stress Styles

Not all stress forms are counterproductive or even negative. Some of the various kinds of stress you may encounter include:

- **Acute stress:** Acute stress is a form of stress that can be either optimistic or more distressing in the very short term; this is the type of stress we experience most frequently in everyday life.
- **Chronic stress:** Chronic stress is stress that appears never-ending and inescapable, such as the stress of a poor marriage or an excessively taxing job; traumatic events and childhood trauma may also result from chronic stress.
- **Episodic acute stress:** Acute stress episodic is acute stress that appears to be rampant and a way of life, generating a life of constant misery.
- **Eustress:** Eustress is thrilling and entertaining. It is referred to as a productive form of stress that will keep you energized. It's related to adrenaline spikes, such as when you're skiing or running to reach a deadline.

## 2.Symptoms of Stress

- **Psychological signs:** such as trouble focusing, anxiety, anxiety, and difficulty recalling
- **Emotional signs:** such as being annoyed, upset, moody, or frustrated
- **Physical symptoms:** such as high blood pressure, weight changes, repeated colds or illnesses, menstrual cycle changes and libido changes, etc.
- **Signs of behavior:** such as bad self-care, not finding time to deal with the things you love, or dependent on drugs and alcohol
- It is not always easy to recognize stress, but there are some ways to recognize some indicators that too much pressure might be encountered.

Figure 1: tfa.org

## 3. Causes of Stress

Stress on the job may have different roots, or come from only one part of the duties of a worker. And its consequences are far-reaching: both employers and their workers may be affected by occupational stress. The economy is presently on the upswing, but in not-so-distant years, job stability was unclear. In companies and enterprises of all sorts, downsizing, layoffs, mergers and bankruptcies take place; this implies major changes for employees. Even where there is no job loss, workers can face increased liability, higher demands for production, reduced benefits, pay cuts and more. This causes an aura of tension around the workplace in general. Some of the known causes of work stress are:

- **Low morale:** Staff often feel helpless when morale is low. This makes them complacent in turn, and productivity suffers. Secretary, waitress, middle manager, police officer, and editor include some of the most difficult jobs. All of these professions are distinguished by the service element of responsibility: these professionals must respond with little influence over events to the demands and timelines of others. Feelings of too little authority, unfair labour conditions and insufficient job descriptions are typical for these types of occupations.
- **Management style:** Management style is another element in difficult job conditions. Staff don't feel valued by their peers and bosses when a workplace has bad contact and employees are not involved in decision-making processes. Moreover, due to the impact on work-life balance, a lack of family-friendly policies can contribute to increased stress.
- **Job responsibilities:** A major contributor to occupational stress is how roles are delegated and carried out. This entails heavy workloads, rare breaks, long hours and transfers, unnecessary routine activities, lacking the expertise of staff, and more. When job expectations are uncertain or conflicting, employees feel they have too much responsibility and too many "hats to wear."
- **Career issues:** Career concerns such as job dissatisfaction or lack of promotion prospects are another factor in occupational stress. Rapid changes are often identified as troublesome, with little to no learning curve.
- **Traumatic events:** It is true that some professions are more dangerous than others, although they are not ideal. Every day, many criminal justice specialists, firefighters, first responders and military members face difficult conditions and personal danger. This can sometimes trigger ordinary responsibilities to become difficult. Positions such as those mentioned above are particularly stressful for that reason.
- **Work climate:** Most of the previous causes of workplace stress are mental, but physical stress may also be caused by a subpar work environment. Whether this is due to noise, lack of privacy, insufficient temperature regulation or inadequate equipment, the work environment is important for minimizing tension in the workplace.

4. **Motivation and Stress Management**

Figure 2: Unique Business Solutions

The fastest growing cause of absence from work is organizational stress. Organizational tension enhances the job output of workers, contributing to better professional outcomes, creating an improvement in the overall organization's competitiveness and profitability. Stress may have a negative effect on the organization's efficiency and competitiveness, and may also increase health insurance costs. Employers should also regard occupational stress as a serious issue and must take steps by stress management systems to avoid workers suffering from stress resulting from their jobs. It is certainly that by improving working conditions and by motivating employees, a company may reach better results in professional performance than any of them.

**Impacts of stress on achievement motivation**
Stress can affect motivation positively. Since stress is triggered by a lack of resources to fulfill those requirements, the desire to improve the effects of stress on the body is helpful in improving the condition in which a person might be. For instance, if a student feels depressed and frustrated by the amount of school work they need to do, instead of remaining in the stressed state, the student may be inspired to relieve themselves from the stressful situation by these feelings. By beginning one piece of evaluation and completing it and finishing the others, the student would be able to complete this one-by-one until they were all done, resulting in decreasing

stress feelings.

**Impacts of achievement motivation on stress**

While stress can have many negative effects on one's motivation for achievement, motivation for achievement itself can also cause levels of stress to increase. The development of unrealistically high expectations for oneself can trigger an increase in stress levels due to the realisation of not being able to meet these expectations. Others' expectations can also lead to an increase in stress levels as the need to reach these expectations in order to fulfill these people and their expectations bring more pressure and therefore more stress and anxiety. In order for stress levels to be managed and sustained, people can build reasonable and achievable expectations and goals for themselves. The targets can be increased after meeting these set goals, pushing the participant harder, making them more difficult before these goals are achieved, and so on. In order for change to be measurable, goals should be set to be practical, raising the motivation of a person.

5.  **Motivation Theories**

- **Maslow's Hierarchy of Needs:** The theory of Maslow depends on the fact that individuals tend to increase what they want to do in life and their desires are prioritized according to their significance. The substance theories of job satisfaction, originating from Maslow's hierarchy of needs, revolve around the needs of workers and the factors that offer them a fair degree of satisfaction. Its hierarchy of needs of Maslow forms the base of theories that aim to describe work satisfaction. Teachers, as all individuals, have needs that must be met. They also need the recognition and appreciation of students, colleagues, and parents, in addition to the basic needs for food, shelter and clothing, protection from physical, harm, and social interaction. Maslow came up with a five-stage theory focused on the basic physical, biological, social and psychological needs of human beings that positions the individual's needs in various categories and prioritizes their achievement. In order of declining priority, these groups are:

- physiological needs (food, shelter, clothing)
- safety and security needs (physical protection)
- social needs (association with others)
- esteem needs (receiving acknowledgement from others)

- Self-actualization needs (the desire for accomplishment or to leave behind a legacy).

- **Herzberg's Two-Factor Theory/Motivator Hygiene:**

- **Hygiene factors-** Hygiene factors are those job factors that are important for workplace motivation to occur. This do not contribute to long-term positive satisfaction. But if these variables are missing or if these variables in the workplace are non-existent, then they lead to frustration. In other words, hygiene variables are those variables that pacify the workers when adequate/reasonable in a job and do not make them unhappy. To function, these variables are extrinsic. Hygiene factors are often referred to as dissatisfies or variables of maintenance as they are required to prevent dissatisfaction. These variables define the work environment/scenario.

i. **Pay** - The arrangement of pay or salary should be suitable and fair. They must be fair and competitive in the same sector as those in the same industry.

ii. **Policies and administrative policies of the company** - The policies of the company should not be too rigid. They need to be equal and transparent. Flexible working time, dress code, breaks, holidays, etc. should be included.

iii. **Fringe benefits** - Health care coverage (mediclaims), benefits for family members, employee support services, etc. can be provided to workers.

iv. **Conditions of physical labor** - The working conditions should be secure, clean and hygienic. The equipment for the work should be modified and maintained well.

v. **Status** - The status of the workers should be familiar and maintained within the company.

vi. **Interpersonal relationships** - Workers should have an appropriate and acceptable relationship with their peers, superiors and subordinates. No aspect of dispute or embarrassment should be present.

vii. **Employment Security** - Workers must be granted job security by the organisation.

- **Motivational factors-** Hygiene factors should not be counted as motivators, according to Herzberg. The motivational variables generate positive satisfaction. These variables are inherent in work. These variables inspire the workers to achieve superior results. Such variables are called fulfillers. There are variables involved in carrying out the job. Employees find these variables inherently satisfying. The motivators symbolized the psychological needs that were viewed as an added gain. Factors that are motivational include:

i. **Recognition** - The workers should be rewarded and appreciated by the executives for their achievements.
ii. **Sense of accomplishment** - The workers must have a sense of accomplishment. This is contingent on the job. In the work, there must be a fruit of some kind.
iii. **Development and promotional opportunities** - In an organisation, there must be opportunities for growth and success to inspire workers to perform well.
iv. **Responsibility** - Workers must be held accountable for the job themselves. The supervisors should give them control of the job. They should reduce power, but maintain responsibility.
v. **Job meaningfulness** - For the employee to succeed and get motivated, the work itself should be meaningful, exciting and difficult.

**Recommendations and Findings**
**1.Eat healthily:**

- Eating healthily can reduce the risks of diet-related diseases
- There is a growing amount of evidence showing how food affects our mood and how eating healthily can improve this
- Protect feelings of wellbeing by ensuring that diet provides adequate amounts of brain nutrients such as essential vitamins and minerals, as well as water

1. **Be aware of smoking and drinking alcohol:**

- Try not to, or reduce the amount of smoke and drink alcohol
- Even though they may seem to reduce tension initially, this is misleading as they often make problems worse

3. **Exercise:**

- Try and integrate physical exercise into your lifestyle as it can be very effective in relieving stress
- Even just going out and getting some fresh air, and taking some light physical exercise, like going for a walk to the shops can really help

Figure 3: randstadriscsmart

## 4. Take time out:

- Take time to relax
- Strike the balance between responsibility to others and responsibility to oneself, this can really reduce stress levels

**Be mindful:**

- Mindfulness is a mind-body approach to life that helps us to relate differently to experiences. It involves paying attention to our thoughts and feelings in a way that increases our ability to manage difficult situations and make wise choices

- Try to practice mindfulness regularly
- Mindfulness meditation can be practised anywhere at any time
- Research has suggested that it can reduce the effects of stress, anxiety and related problems such as insomnia, poor concentration and low moods, in some people

Figure 4: yummy mummy club

6. **Get some restful sleep**
7. **Don't be too hard on yourself**

- Try to keep things in perspective.
- Remember that having a bad day is a universal human experience
- When your inner critic or an outer critic finds faults, try and find truth and exception to what is being said
- Take a few minutes each day to appreciate yourself

## Conclusion

Job stress management implies learning to treat situations differently but it also means learning how to treat oneself, understanding one's strengths, and making better use of one's personal skills. It depends not only on external circumstances but on our way of perceiving and interpreting them, to know how to handle stress at work or in any professional and personal sense. In this age of Confusion, everyone in today's workplace seems to be under more strain. Study after study shows that it is an increasing challenge to handle stress. Typically, people think of stress as something totally negative, but as we have seen, when properly handled, stress has real benefits. Again, the crucial challenge for executives is to develop a greater understanding of stress in the workplace, in their organisations, and in their teams and employees. The issue of stress should be monitored by everyone in a position of organizational or team leadership. In general, by enhancing employee autonomy, preparation, working conditions, schedules, career growth, support structures, effective management practices would likely minimize unnecessary stress.

# CHAPTER FIVE

# Stress Management At Workplace And At Home: Homoeopathic Approach Towards Stress

**Introduction**

Our body gives response to stressor and will produce stress. Stress can be of 2 types physical add mental . Physical is called somatic & mental called psychosomatic. Every human need to adopt the change in internal and external environment. And if a person fails to adopt then leads to psychosomatic diseases. Many people assume that psychosomatic diseases does not exist but according to theory of PNE(Pituitary- Neuro- Endocrine) axis if there is a disturbance in this axis leads to diseased conditions. Various ups and downs at the mental level triggers physiological stress response and this stress leads to psychosomatic disorders if the body refuses to manage due to low immunity. Many people complaining of sleeplessness, decreased appetite, sudden weight gain, tightness or pain in chest region etc these are the some examples of stress response if it prolongs then pathophysiological changes occurs at cell level.

Sources of the stress are many some of them are frustrations, failures, loss of loved ones, financial loss, conflicts, failure of achieving targets at work place, job targets, marital stress, relationship stress, too much travelling for long distances etc

Any human being who will come across with such type of negative stimulus gives alarming response at start that is initiation of increase heart rate, temperature, adrenalin levels in other words physiological response is called fight or flight reaction. Once the stress situation is over homeostasis returns but when it fails leads to various types of permanent changes in the form of psychosomatic diseases. Stress can be at workplace and as well as at home.

At home many types of stress can be encountered such as financial management, children behaviour, marital relations not going smoothly, neighbourhood etc. In chronic cases of management of stress our body does not respond to natural defence mechanisms. Adaptability is lost in such conditions and now the person develops certain disease conditions commonest is hypertension, diabetes, renal stones etc.

Management of stress is depending on individual's choice and mainly time period for which person suffers from stress. Acute or short time stress is good according physiological effects and will help individual to complete goals or targets. But chronic stress will be harmful to body as body stops giving defence response to stressors. In short the persons coping capacity with stress is over, now at this time body will show some signs and symptoms called alarming sings and symptoms.

But human tendency is to neglect such alarming symptoms. Therefore disease conditions will be coming up in some forms for example high blood pressure, diabetes, hypothyroidism, hyperthyroidism, menstrual complaints, poly cystic ovarian diseases, infertility, etc.

So to avoid all these person who are experiencing acute phases of stress on and off should practice yoga, or meditation, or exercise. Performing at least one of these will definitely help the persons. And instead doing all preventive measures if its uncontrolled then he or she can take help of any pathy. Here role of homoeopathy comes as homoeopathy offers very good and safe results.

**Types of management stress --**

Stress is our psychological and physiological reaction to an event or condition that is considered a threat or challenge.

We most commonly refer to stress as a feeling of emotional pressure and strain when we feel unable to cope or are overwhelmed by something.

When we experience stress, our bodies react by releasing a surge of chemicals and hormones throughout our bodies. This triggers the fight-or-flight response that many of us are familiar with.

But it also affects numerous other systems within us, including our metabolism, memory, and immune system. Under normal circumstances, our mental, emotional, and physical state should return to normal once the stressful event has passed. This is where our mental fitness comes into play. While small amounts of positive stress can help us perform better, the key is that this stress is brief. Acute and prolonged stress may lead to long-term health problems and exacerbate existing conditions.

moolihai.com

At any place try to identify stressors or that triggering factor, after identify if you cannot remove it then try to control inner state. Perhaps the most direct way to do this is meditation, yoga, exercise, going out with friends, staying positive, promoting healthy work schedule, along with all this good eating habits add biological cycles of sleeping that will definitely help in reducing stress.

After identify if you cannot remove it try to control inner state of mind perhaps the most direct way to do this is meditation, yoga, Exercise, going out with friends, staying positive, promoting healthy work schedule, along with all this good eating habits will definitely help in reducing stress.

verywellmind.com

**Yoga** acts as a great stress buster. It helps in respiratory movements concentration, relaxations of body and many other benefits.

Some of the techniques of yoga such as **PRANAYAM** helps in controlling breath movement which increases the awareness of breath and which ultimately relaxes body by taking deep breaths. Pranayama also helps to increase vital capacity and tidal volume of lungs, which ultimately helps in good oxygenation. Good oxygenation keeps us fresh and happy. Many researches have proven that SURYANAMASKAR is helpful for blood circulation, overall maintenance of cardiovascular system. One more positive point of performing yoga in early morning is person feels fresh all day, sense of relaxation in stress full conditions, increased ability of work done, and positive attitude towards difficult situations.

Persons who practices yoga for years together has better life style, better way of maintain homoeostasis. In today's fast moving world younger generations are suffering from cardiovascular diseases due to lack of exercise. Young generation's eating habits are at fault which also leads to different diseases. Therefore awareness of exercise or yoga is needed for young as well as old generations.

Next relaxation session of yoga is **SHAWASAN** (like a corpse) or YOGA –NIDRA. If we spend at least 5 to 10 minutes daily then it will be a relaxing session and also act as a great stress reducer. By doing BHUJANGAASAN gives strength to back bone, good blood circulation to abdominal organs, and also helps in relieving stress. BALASAN (like child) helps to relax back, thorax and neck muscles along with the consciousness of breathing. BHRAMARI is like bee like sound gives instant calming effect, also lowers blood pressure, it is observed that it is best breathing exercise for mind agitation.

Now a days many physicians are using **pet therapy**. Pet therapy is a guided interaction between person and trained animal. Dogs and cats are commonly used in pet therapy. Type of animal can be chosen according to the person's like. Researchers claimed that pet therapy is useful in mentally as well as physically challenged persons. These furry coats friends acts magically to reduce tension or stress of person. It can help to reduce blood pressure and overall improvement of cardiovascular health. It also helps in reduction in intensity of pain, and improves psychological state of wellbeing. A special bonding will be built in between that pet and the person. For children who are born and brought up with one pet at home they have more capability of handling stress full conditions as compared to other children. Most of persons are unaware of benefits of pet at home. Dogs are best examples for these. They are man's best companions. They can understand many emotions of us. They observe our body language or changed tone of voice and try to react accordingly. Many dog owners experienced that like human being dogs look into our eyes and try to interpret our emotional turmoil. On top of all one thing pets gives us is unconditional love. This unconditioned love is most crucial part of getting cured. In this fast moving world nobody has time for any one. So pets are the best treatment or option to treat stress.

Everyone let it be at any age requires exercise. Exercise is the next stress buster. Benefits we receive from exercise are maintaining mental fitness, reducing fatigue, increase in concentration, improves alertness, Enhancing overall cognitive functions. Exercise or any favourite physical activity produces endorphin in brain which acts as a natural painkiller and helps in reducing stress during painful conditions. Simple walking for everyday for 30 minutes releases tension from bigger muscles such as calf muscle thigh muscles, deepening of breath and quietening effects on nervous system. Dancing is the best exercise which will be creative as well as reducing stress.

Unlike pet therapy next level **stress buster is gardening**. When the person comes in contact with various plants , beautiful flowers, earth, nature, that increases your concentration and more of when we see budding plants gives immense pleasure and satisfaction for our work done. In such kind of work we divert our energy in doing fruitful work ultimately reducing stress at home or at workplace. Benefits of growing plants are you are exposed to sunlight which gives you vitamin D. Now this vitamin D helps to strengthen bones. In some cases of gardening shows creative mind, means indoor gardening will gives immensely beautiful house decoration. All these activities reduces cortisol levels. Cortisol is one of stress producing hormone. Another benefit is growing our own food which ultimately gives relaxation and work which is full of fun.

**Music** is another entity which plays a very good role in management of the stress. Playing a piano or playing a flute or sitar and listening to the favourite music will definitely releases feel good hormones and the ultimate result is quietening of the nervous system. Singing song or listening to music acts as soothing effect on stressful mind.

**Practice of meditation** also released the stress The process of meditation involves setting in relaxed position focusing and concentrating on the one thought and pronunciation of one word for example "oommmm". With the practice of controlling breath, that is time of inspiration and time of expiration is prolonged so that Physiology of the oxygenation is done in very good manner and when oxygenation of each cell tissue is enhanced automatically body feels refreshed and quieting effect comes down very fast. Meditation is old school practice. Many researchers have shown that those who practice meditation regularly is more capable of recovering from stressful situations and experience least stress as do they face challenges in day today life.

**Homoeopathic Approach Towards Stress--**

If above auxiliary line of treatment is not sufficient then comes role of medicines. Different pathies have different role in management of stress.

In homeopathy there are many remedies for management of stress. Common remedies such as Aconite, Arsenic Album, Pulsatilla, Lycopodium, Silicia, Stramonium, Calcarea Carb, Kali Phos are few examples.

But homeopathic treatment is given according to constitution of that patient. Constitution is nothing but physical and mental makeup of that Individual. Individualisation means no two personalities are same. Example for this is, if two different persons are coming with same disease, but both of them require different homoeopathic remedies according to their constitution. So treating stress in two different persons requires different homoeopathic medicines as per their constitution.

As stress is also harming health at dynamic level, PNE axis will be easily is disturbed in stressful conditions, this balance will be nicely maintained by homoeopathic drugs. Homoeopathic medicines are acting at dynamic levels. Vital force will be stabilised and homoeostasis is regained. Now to treat the vital force at dynamic level, we require medicine which will be acting at dynamic state. To achieve this theory of drug dynamization is useful to introduce medicine in patients.

Drug dynamization is the process where potentization of medicine is done to evolve hidden curative power of that drug. Now this dose of homeopathic medicine will be acting on psychosomatic level, which was disturbed during stress or stressful conditions or in stress situations. Correct constitutional homeopathic medicine is helpful to regain health state. With the help of homoeopathic constitutional medicine also helps in rebuilding of immunity. Homeostatic level of the person is regained by practicing regular sessions of yoga, regular exercise, good eating and sleeping habits. Stress can be managed at any level may it be at office or may it at home.

**Recurring episodes of stress on and off will be reduced by homoeopathic medicines such as-**

medicalnewstoday.com

**Aconite--**

Intense fear, sudden anxiety, panic attacks, dry mouth. Fear of death.

**Calcerea carb--**

Sluggish, passive personality, fair chubby blond look, enlarged and hard lymphatic glands, chilly patient, fear of mental confusion, disposition to weep even at trifles, easily frightened and offended, fear of death and fear of being ill. Aversion to all mental work. Absence of will power. Weakness of memory and of conception, with difficulty in thinking. Dizziness of mind. Tendency to make mistakes in speaking. She fears she will lose her concentration, or that people will observe her confusion of mind. Forgetful, confused low spirited.

**Kali Phos--**

Anguish, stress can not be managed, depressed state of mind & body, nervous, hot, easily startled, trembling of hands due to nervousness, can not recollect words, mind is very sluggish, exhaustion after slightest mental exertion, sleeplessness during later part of night, sleeplessness from mental exertion, weak memory.

**Arsenicum Album—**

If the person is mentally & physically restless, anxiety about small things, burning is also one of key feature of this remedy. Screaming in painful conditions, fear of alone is also marked feature of arsenic album.

**Pulsatilla—**

Thirstless remedy, changeability, weeping mood, mild , gentle , affectionate persons. Pulsatilla patient is sad tearful mild calm and quiet personality easily disturbed by change.

**Lycopodium--**

Mentally lycopodium patient is very tired chronic fatigue often faces forgetfulness he has aversion towards undertaking new activity a Virgin for appearing in a new role he always fears something will bad happen fear of appearing in public place

**Silicia—**

Fear of dread of appearing in public but once starts get a nice command on the subject. Silicia is a chilly patient, very peculiar kind of state of mind dread of failure. Self confidence is lacking, stamina is lacking.

**Stramonium--**

Cant bear solitude, fear of ghost, loquacious, religious mania, can not bear shining object, stammering speech, dry mouth, fear of darkness.

**Conclusion—**

In this modern fast moving era though stress is a very common condition and can be dealt smartly along with practice of yoga, practice of meditation, regular exercise, good eating habits and maintaining biological cycles (sleep) will definitely reduce amount of stress in our life. If the stressors are too long and persistent then old age people will be more vulnerable to psychosomatic disorders. Our own immunity is good fighter for acute stressors but sometimes therapeutic management is required to maintain homeostasis. Homeoapathy provides holistic approach towards such cases of stress as it cures gently and permanently. Homeoapathic treatment also enhances immunity of the patients. So Management of stress is not a big deal unless until we try to solve it willingly. As it is said that one man's food is another man's poison, which means stress is triggering some good physiological changes in some persons but can produce some pathological changes in some persons. If not managed by body's own defence mechanisms then cell or tissue level pathological changes are observed. Acute stress can be easily managed and does not produce any harm to body but chronic that is long lasting stress are harmful and requires traditional medicinal line of treatment along with the auxiliary line of treatment. Will power of the person is also playing very important role in managing the stress.

# CHAPTER SIX

# Stress Management in our lives with the help of Education and Technology etc Strategies

**Introduction:**

What Is Stress?

Stress is your body's response to changes in your life. Because life involves constant change—ranging from everyday, routine changes like commuting from home to work to adapt to major life changes like marriage, divorce, or death of a loved one—there is no avoiding stress.1

Your goal shouldn't be to eliminate all stress but to eliminate unnecessary stress and effectively manage the rest. There are some common causes of stress that many people experience, but each person is different.

**Causes:**

Stress can come from many sources, which are known as "stressors." Because our experience of what is considered "stressful" is created by our unique perceptions of what we encounter in life (based on our own mix of personality traits, available resources, and habitual thought patterns), a situation may be perceived as "stressful" by one person and merely "challenging" by someone else. We all experience stress in our lives. Because the vast majority of health problems are caused or influenced by stress, it's important to understand how stress affects your body and learn effective stress management techniques to make stress work for you rather than against you.

Simply put, one person's stress trigger may not register as stressful to someone else. That said, certain situations tend to cause more stress in most people and can increase the risk of burnout. For example, when we find ourselves in situations where there are high demands on us but we little control and few choices, we are likely to experience stress. We might also feel stress when we don't feel equipped; where we may be harshly judged by others; and where consequences for failure are steep or unpredictable. Many people are stressed by their jobs, relationships, financial issues, and health problems, as well as more mundane things like clutter or busy schedules. Learning skills to cope with these stressors can help reduce your experience of stress.

**Stress Management:**

Stress can be effectively managed in many different ways. The best stress management plans usually include a mix of stress relievers that address stress physically and psychologically and help to develop resilience and coping skills.

**5.0 8 Ways Technology Can Reduce Stress:**

It can be argued that technology has added some stress to our lives. In our professional and social lives, innovation has made it easier to connect with other people – but this can be a blessing and a curse. Does technology help with stress...or is it just causing it?

With laptops, smart phones, and tablets, we are only a call, text, or email away from the demands of our business, long after "normal" business hours have ended. We can sign contracts, deliver sales proposals, or communicate with clients, staff, or employers 24/7. With these tools literally at our fingertips, taking time off to focus on yourself, family, friends, or hobbies can be challenging. Our social lives can be filled with the pressure of "keeping up," amplified by access to social media sites that are constantly reminding us that our peers are living their best lives, or at least acting like it in photos they post. For people vulnerable to feelings of isolation or loneliness, it's easy to lose perspective.

While innovation might be to blame for some extra anxiety in our lives, we can certainly turn the tables on it and use technology to our advantage. Cutting-edge advances in technology can be used to help us reduce stress, form positive interpersonal connections, and encourage mental and emotional health. Let's explore some of the ways technology helps with stress.

Stress relief technology comes in many forms, from apps to online games and social media, and everyone has unique needs. The great news is that technology allows you to try these different methods in the comfort of your own home, sitting on a train during a long commute, or during your lunch hour. If you are feeling stressed or anxious, you may get some relief from tools available on mobile devices you can use regardless of where you are.

Reducing stress in our daily lives is important for our overall physical and mental health. Reports show a connection between stress and many illnesses. Chronic stress can lower your immune system (making it easier to get sick), raise your blood pressure (leading to heart disease), cause insomnia, and lead to obesity, substance abuse, and depression. While it may be impossible to eliminate stress completely from our lives, there are ways to use some of the innovative technology on the market to help reduce stress and encourage relaxation.

Try a few of the following ways to use technology to reduce stress and stay healthy:

**i) Wearable Tech:**

You may be familiar with products like FitBit and Apple Watch for their physical fitness tracking, but did you know that some of the wearable fitness gadgets on the market can actually help you relax? Apple Watch Series 3 can help you focus on your breathing by replicating a calming breathing rhythm with small vibrating buzzes, while Garmin Vivosport can provide a guided breathing exercise to help center yourself when your heart rate variability (HRV) sensor shows your heart rate and stress level rising. If you thought that wearables only go on your wrist, you might be surprised to learn about Vitali's "smart bra" that will track your HRV and posture, and help identify what triggers stress for you.

**ii) Scheduled Meditation:**

The word "meditation" may conjure images of sitting peacefully on a rock in a field of flowers, taking a vow of silence while you commune with nature, but in today's world, it can simply be a calming technique during a stressful day or week. Products from companies like Muse will use your brain activity to train you to relax, identify distractions, and teach you how to apply calming techniques to your daily routine. Headspace, a tech company started by a former Buddhist monk trained in meditation across the globe, offers a smartphone app with guided-themed meditation sessions that can fit into your hectic day and can help you deal with stress.

**iii) YouTube:**

While less than positive content can be found on any site that allows the public to post videos, YouTube can actually be a great source of humour, music, and positive imagery. A few minutes of watching content that makes you laugh or reminds us of the compassion and love that exists in the world can help you escape from an otherwise stressful day and hit the restart button on your mood. Whether you enjoy listening to a comedian who finds hilarity in everyday struggles or finds yourself relaxing as you listen to undiscovered artists or musicians, videos on YouTube can be short and sweet, but can help you take a breath and make you smile long enough to let go of some of the stress you are feeling.

**iv) Anxiety Management:**

Anxiety can be challenging, but technology can help you understand and manage it. The SAM app helps monitor your anxiety and behaviour, and can connect you anonymously with a community of support and shared experience. Getting support can help alleviate feelings of isolation as you find common ground with other people with similar challenges.

**v) Social Media:**

Despite being a double-edged sword, social media sites like Face book, Instagram, and Twitter can actually help you stay connected with friends and loved ones, leading to better mental and emotional health. While these sites can certainly become hubs of peer pressure, unrealistic expectations, and, unfortunately, bullying for teens, older adults with limited mobility can benefit from the social interaction provided through these sites. Family pages can be created on Face book, for instance, to help maintain connections with loved ones even when people are spread out across the country. Local community center pages and support groups on Face book and Twitter can notify you about opportunities to get involved in your community and find people you share similar interests with.

**vi) Online Fitness:**

Physical and mental fitness often goes hand-in-hand, and thanks to sites like Daily Burn, you don't have to go to a gym or purchase expensive equipment. With access to over a hundred 30-minute workouts, you can try a variety of routines for just $15/month. Many celebrity trainers, including Tracy Anderson and Jillian Michaels, offer online streaming subscriptions that will make you feel like you have a personal trainer in the comfort of your own home. Feeling strong, active, and healthy can contribute to mental wellness, reduce the affects of stress, and keep you feeling more balanced and relaxed throughout the day.

**vii) Relaxing Online Games:**

Let's face it – some video games are just not relaxing. They require concentration, and quick reflexes, and can make you anxious as you try to beat the clock. Fortunately, there are some online games that will help reduce stress. Games like Little Wheel and Echogenesis create relaxing digital worlds with beautiful, calming graphics. Games like Pigment give you access to a digital version of adult colouring books that have gained popularity recently. Colouring has been known to reduce stress, enhance concentration, and help you practice mindfulness.

**viii) Lifestyle Technology:**

Don't underestimate the ways that technology helps with stress in our home, or when we are away from it. Make life less stressful with innovative smart-home tools, including security cameras, safety monitors, or even a "smart" washing machine or refrigerator. Anything that makes your life easier or puts your mind at ease while you are away from your home can reduce stress in your daily life.

If you are like most of us and experience stress in your daily life, consider the benefits and ease of stress relief technology. With access to wellness programs, meditations, games, and online ways to connect with the people you care about, you may find ways to use technology to reduce stress and help you feel more relaxed. If your anxiety or stress continues and is affecting your physical or mental health, please discuss your concerns with your physician as soon as possible.

**HOW TO USE TECHNOLOGY TO DE-STRESS:**

While research suggests technology may cause anxiety, other studies argue technology could help manage everyday stresses. Continue reading to learn how to take advantage of today's technology in order to relax.

**i) DOWNLOAD STRESS-RELIEVING APPS:**

While research suggests technology may cause anxiety, other studies argue technology could help manage everyday stresses. Continue reading to learn how to take advantage of today's technology in order to relax.

While using technology can make some feel stressed, others find relief in certain apps that are designed to help users unwind. According to Statista, there are about 2 million apps to choose from in the App Store. From mood tracking to squeezing a virtual rubber duck, there's an app for almost any type of stress relief you're searching for. Instead of scrolling through social media and creating more negative energy, utilize apps such as Personal Zen, which contains a series of games focused on reducing anxiety levels.

### ii) PRACTICE FITBIT AND APPLE WATCH BREATHING EXERCISES:

Most of today's technology has built-in stress-relieving features for our benefit. If you own a FitBit or Apple Watch, try the breathing exercise features to relieve stress. Wearable technology can track when you're stressed so you can learn to anticipate negative emotions and use features such as breathing exercises to calm down. If you don't own a wearable, search for apps in the App Store or watch videos on YouTube to simulate breathing exercises.

### iii) CREATE A SMART HOME:

Building a smart home can reduce the time you spend worrying about chores and keeping up with daily tasks. Create a chore chart with Amazon Alexa to keep track of what's already been done and what still needs to be done around the house. Smart devices are created to connect to other smart devices to make your life easier. From turning off the lights to helping you find your phone, creating a smart home can help eliminate everyday stress.

### iv) FOLLOW FITNESS VIDEOS:

Exercise is a popular stress reliever and is easier than ever to add to your routine due to the availability of virtual fitness classes. Working out releases endorphins, which lowers stress levels. Try following videos of fitness classes such as Zumba or yoga to find the perfect workout and let off some steam.

### v) CREATE A SMART HOME:

Building a smart home can reduce the time you spend worrying about chores and keeping up with daily tasks. Create a chore chart with Amazon Alexa to keep track of what's already been done and what still needs to be done around the house. Smart devices are created to connect to other smart devices to make your life easier. From turning off the lights to helping you find your phone, creating a smart home can help eliminate everyday stress.

### vi) STREAM RELAXING MUSIC:

Listening to music is one of the most common ways to relieve stress since it requires minimal effort. Listen to your favorite songs to de-stress, or listen to the top 10 relaxing songs ranked by scientists if you're in need of immediate relaxation. For some, silence increases anxiety levels, but for others, too much noise can create more stress. If a room filled with music causes chaos for you, try using a white noise machine or streaming white noise online. Using white noise to block out any unnecessary and loud noises can also increase productivity as well as reduce stress.

### vii) ENSURE YOUR DATA IS SECURE:

While keeping your data secure may not be one of your main stressors, taking steps to ensure your personal information is safe can be reassuring. New viruses and threats emerge every day, so make sure your antivirus software is up-to-date on your computer and change your passwords to all of your online accounts at least once a year to avoid getting hacked. Keep stress at bay by taking steps to keep you and your family's or business' information safe.

If technology is causing you stress instead of helping you de-stress, enlist the help of your local Computer Troubleshooters office! Our tech professionals are ready to help secure your network to ensure you won't stress over technology.

**WHY YOU NEED TO MANAGE YOUR STRESS:**

The ability to manage your stress is an important skill to have as stress can negatively impact a host of different areas in your life including work, relationships, health and body functioning. When your stress is well managed it's likely that you don't think about challenges too much when they occur, as you are prepared to tackle them emotionally, physically and psychologically. If your stress is unmanaged though, these difficulties can seem overwhelming and insurmountable.

Stress can be inescapable; it's a part of modern life with all of the responsibilities we have. Here are the top 5 reasons to manage your stress:

**i) Health:**

Stress has a quantifiable impact on your body and health. According to the American Psychological Association, stress can impact the whole entire body from the musculoskeletal system to the reproductive system. Chronic pain disorders can be brought on or aggravated by stress. Stress is found to be a component of heart disease, diabetes, ulcers, impotence and a decreased sexual drive. Stress can cause emotional eating and a lack of motivation or energy to exercise and maintain healthy behaviors. Managing your stress can mean a longer, happier and healthier life.

**ii) Work:**

Stress at work is a reality. There is unlikely to be any career without some form of stress, however, if chronic stress is mounting at your job, it could have some real consequences. Chronic stress at work can lead to decreased productivity, being skipped over for raises or advancements and impaired work relationships. Managing your stress where you likely spend the vast majority of your waking hours can make you a better employee, co-worker or supervisor.

### iii) Parenting:

Parenting is hard. There is no parent on the planet who doesn't experience some level of stress. Being able to manage your stress can make you a more effective and happier parent. When you are able to utilize stress reduction exercises, you are better able to teach your children how to manage their stress too. Managing your stress gives you more patience, tolerance and able to handle all the challenges that come with raising children.

### iv) Relationships:

When you are stressed, your relationships will most certainly be impacted. It's difficult to spend time with loved ones when you are overwhelmed by stress. One is more likely to fight or argue as a response to their own stress rather than communicate effectively with their partners. Relationships suffer if stress remains unmanaged.

### v) Overall Level of Happiness:

Chronic stress can greatly increase the likelihood of developing symptoms of depression, anxiety, or other mental health difficulties. When one manages their stress, they experience less frustration with life's challenges, decreased worries about the future and have an improved sense of well-being. Being able to manage stress through utilizing effective coping skills and stress management techniques can make you a happier and healthier individual.

Stress may feel inescapable and perhaps it is, but you are not alone in facing your challenges. It is possible to learn how to manage your stress. Reach out today to learn more about how reducing your stress will help improve your life.

### How Technology Can Help to Prevent Workplace Stress:

We spend over eight hours a day, five days a week at work. Some of us may even spend more of our waking hours with our colleagues than our families. It's therefore important that our working lives leave us happy and fulfilled.

Too much pressure or long-term stress can cause employees to burn out, leaving them with less energy to function in and out of work. Too little work – or a lack of stimulation – can also lead to stress. Employees feel under-fulfilled, like they're wasting their time, and want to be anywhere but at work. The more stressed employees are, the less work they get done, and the more businesses suffer. Embracing technological innovations puts employees back in control of how they spend their time at work and greatly reduces the risks of stress and burnout.

**Here are four ways technology can make employees feel more fulfilled, and help to prevent workplace stress.**

**i) Organize and coordinate schedules:**

Trying to find a time when a team can meet to discuss something important can often take as long – sometimes even longer – than the meeting itself. If it's an important or last-minute meeting, trying to get everyone together can cause employees huge amounts of stress.

There's always a risk of someone being double-booked because they didn't check their calendar before agreeing to a suggested time. This then causes more stress because the meeting needs to be rescheduled.

Calendar connectivity means that this process can be automated, preventing double bookings and avoiding any stress the process could cause. Instead of long email chains or back-and-forth phone calls, the person organizing the meeting can tell the software whom they need in the meeting. It can then suggest a list of times when everyone is free to meet. If calendars are set up for bookable resources such as meeting rooms or parking spaces, it can incorporate this into its calculations too. Connecting an employees' calendar to HR software also means that they don't need to switch between applications to keep track of their schedules.

**ii) Speed up and streamline complicated processes:**

On the surface, organizing interviews seems like an easy process, but with so many candidates and interview panelists to coordinate, it quickly becomes laborious. Hiring managers can spend as many as 20 hours a month organizing interviews. Automating this process gives hiring managers more time to spend on other tasks, saves interview panelists from having to constantly flit between their calendar and emails, and allows candidates to book their interviews discreetly.

Another process that can be automated is the organization of staff appraisals. In large organizations, this process can be particularly time-consuming. However, when employees are calendar connected, the software can work out the best times for an employee to meet their manager and automatically add the appointments to their calendar. No matter what size their team is, the process is instant. Offering training programs for employees to expand their skills further breaks up the tedium of the daily routine. Training programs don't just have to take place at work, either. There are thousands of online courses out there, and many of them are free. Many industries also have their own courses or week-long events that employees can attend to network and get a change of scenery. Giving employees new ways to learn and grow helps to spark new ideas that they can bring back to the workplace. Learning new skills is also an effective way to prevent stagnation and keep employees interested in their work.

**iii) Monitor employee wellbeing:**

Looking after employees is a key part of HR. New technology means HR teams can track how employees feel and gain insight into how different teams work. They can also encourage employees to get up and get moving by offering incentives such as fitness trackers. Communication tools such as Slack give employees the opportunity to keep in touch whether they work in the same building or in different parts of the country. Tools like this can be key for managers and HR staff to keep informed of how employees are getting along, particularly if they work remotely full- or part-time.

**iv) Let employees take control of their schedules:**

The more things a person has floating around in their mind, the more difficult it is for them to organize their thoughts. When employees have a lot to do and nowhere to organize their time, it's inevitable that something will be forgotten. Taking advantage of technology allows them to use it for everything from creating to-do lists in Trello to tracking customer queries in Zendesk. Giving employees somewhere they can make a note of everything they have to do means that they spend less time trying to remember everything and more time getting things done.

**V) The technology you provide for your employee's matters:**

Richard Branson once said that if you "look after your staff. They'll look after your customers. It's that simple." When employees feel overwhelmed or overworked, they're less productive and less able to help a business to grow. Employees are what make a business a success. Choosing the right people is crucial, but that's only part of it. If you don't look after them, they won't be as good to your business as they could be. By nurturing employees, making them feel appreciated, and giving them opportunities to learn and grow, it not only benefits them, but the business, too. The more knowledge employees acquire in their industry, the more they can use this to create a better customer experience and increase company revenue. This then means the company can grow and increase its profits faster.

**10 Ways to Use Technology for a Healthy And Less-stressful Life:**

Technology is, of course, a double-edged sword. Where the technology can cause a constant state of distraction, anxiety and sleep dysregulation; it can also help us organize our life better, stay healthy and reduce stress caused by today's fast-moving world.

Technology has forever changed the world we live in. We're online, in one way or another, all day long. In our personal and professional lives, technology can be a blessing as it made it easier to connect with others, and a curse that being in a state of always-connected and 24/7 contactable can make it really challenging to take some time to focus on your own well-being or spend time with family and friends. The good news is that we can turn the tables on the dark side of technology by using technology to our advantage to de-stress and relieve some of the anxiety from our hectic lifestyle.

I am going to share 10 effective methods that we teach our staff at iDesignYours where technology can help de-stress and develop a healthy lifestyle.

**i) Decrease the Effects of Blue Light:**

Devices like smartphones, tablets, laptops emit an artificial blue light and staring at screens of our devices all day can cause eye strain, and prevent us from feeling relaxed and sleepy.

a) For your computers, use an app Flux at night to slowly decrease your computer's blue glow like the sunsets.

b) Buy a glare-reducing protective screen cover.

iii. iPhone users can use Night Shift (under Settings > Display) and the less-known Color Tint feature.

c) Android users can download Twilight for their screen-dimming needs.

**ii. Examine Your Phone Time and Reduce It:**

Use Google's Digital Wellbeing for Android Devices that not only chart what you do and for how long, but also packs extra features like turning the screen gray at night to remind you to put your phone down, or it even outright disables apps after a set time. Apple users can use Screen Time that allows you to monitor how much time you spend using your device and what you're doing with it.

**iii. Reduce Noise:**

Numerous studies have linked noise pollution to increased anxiety, depression, high blood pressure, heart disease, and stroke. A Cardiologist at Johannes Gutenberg University in Mainz, Germany says that noise aggravates these health conditions by inducing higher levels of stress.

a.   You can use apps like Krisp to mute background noise During calls.

b.  You can also use noise cancellation and isolation devices that help you relax and sleep better.

**iv) Organize your Life:**

Organizing your time, to-do lists, scheduling events, emails and even going paperless can help you reduce the level of stress in your life. Use these simple apps to organize your life with ease:

i.  OneNote – Organize all your ideas, notes in one place.

ii) Google Calendar – Organize your meetings, events, reminders

iii) Plan – It automatically creates weekly agendas just for your tasks.

iv) Remember the Milk is good for people with lots to remember both at work and at home.

**v) Take Regular Breaks:**

a) You can make your computer or mobile device remind you to practice good work ergonomics and break habits with these apps.

b) Out is a macOS app for break management.

c) Break Timer is a Chrome addon and is available in the Chrome Web Store. It allows you to customize the length of your work and break periods.

d) Eye Care 20 20 20 is an app for iOS and Android that uses the 20-20-20 rule recommended for preventing eye strain: Every 20 minutes take 20 seconds to look at something 20 feet away.

**vi) Make Use of Wearables:**

Fitness products like FitBit and Apple Watch can also help you relax. If you own a FitBit, Apple Watch or Garmin VivoSport, try the guided breathing exercise features to relieve stress when your heart rate variability (HRV) sensor shows your heart rate and stress level rising. If you thought that wearables only go on your wrist, you might be surprised to learn about Vitali's "smart bra" that will track your HRV and posture, and help identify what triggers stress for you.

**vii) Stress Relieving Apps:**

It is said that nowadays there is an app for everything. It is quite true. From mood tracking to squeezing a virtual rubber duck, there's an app or a game for almost any type of stress relief you're searching for.

Instead of scrolling through social media and creating more negative energy, utilize apps/games such as Little Wheel, Echogenesis, Pigment or Personal Zen, which contains a series of games focused on reducing anxiety levels

**viii) Stream Relaxing Music:**

Music is considered the best food for your spirit. Listen to your favorite songs to de-stress, or listen to the top 10 relaxing songs ranked by scientists if you're in need of immediate relaxation.

**ix) Dissolve Your Stress with Meditation:**

Meditation is one of the oldest techniques in the world to relieve stress and tension. Schedule 10 minutes out of each day, put it in your phone's calendar for a reminder, to clear your mind and reset your thought process. If you feel like you are always on the go, try an app like Simple Habit to develop a practice of meditation in the midst of the busyness of life (during a commute, on a walk, while working).

**The Benefits of Stress Management for Employees:**

The discussion has been about the effects of stress at work, but we'd like to turn the focus to the benefits of a low-stress work environment.

**i) Strong company culture:**

Employees have a major role in a company's culture. Healthier employees operating under manageable levels of stress will be happier and more positive, helping to maintain a strong, healthy workplace culture that's conducive to creativity and productivity.

**ii) Less sick days:**

Stress is one of the leading causes of absenteeism in the workplace. Not only will less stress in the workplace result in less "mental health days," but it will also reduce the amount of sick days taken by employees due to a weakened immune system as a result of excessive stress.

**iii) Employee retention & talent acquisition:**

Employees who aren't overly stressed are much more likely to stick around, and prospective employees are much more likely to work for an employer that promotes a low-stress work environment and takes the initiative to help keep their employees healthy.

**iv) It shows you care:**

Actively working to reduce stress through measures like stress management programs and policy shows that you care about your employees and their health and happiness.

Often, stress isn't a company-wide issue, but there will always be individuals going through highly stressful times. One way to help individuals in need is to provide them with resources to better handle their stress to get through those times.

**Conclusion:**

For better or worse, our smartphones, tablets, and computers are here to stay so why not try to harness cutting edge advances in technology to combat the anxiety and stress, and encourage mental and emotional health.

While these tips are useful for reducing the stress associated with everyday technology use, technology addictions are a growing problem, and they sometimes require more serious treatment. According to psychologist and Greatist Expert Dr. Michael Mantell, symptoms of technology addiction include losing track of time or getting angry if your online time is interrupted with real-life activities; turning to online activities to cope with lack of affection or sex; and hearing friends say that they see you more in virtual reality than in real life. Those who suspect they might be suffering from these kinds of problems might seek out cognitive-behavioral therapy, family therapy, or other kinds of counselingTrusted Source

In general, as stressful as modern technology might be, it's unrealistic to think that we can hide from it forever. Luckily, there are lots of ways to stay sane, even while plugged in.Remember: Technology doesn't automatically make us stressed. It's all about how we handle it. So redesign your desk space, create an email-checking schedule, and know that technology is meant to improve your life—not ruin it!

# CHAPTER SEVEN

# An Analysis on Stress Management

**Introduction**

Stress! Ah, stress! We know it, we feel it, and we put up with it sometimes. Our modern life's pace never ceases to quicken, and the world we live in is becoming more complex. In our society, stress, particularly work-related stress, is a rising phenomenon and undoubtedly affects all fields and all occupational groups. It is important for fitness, balance and happiness to learn to handle stress efficiently at work or at home. Corporate success is often influenced by the negative implications of stress on health and individual capacity. It has been called the modern "new evil." The response of the body to environmental constraints is stress.

It can also be defined as a syndrome for dealing with a variety of emotional, physiological, mental or social disorders. Work stress is present in several forms today: standards of success, disputes, workload, lack of time, lack of autonomy, work environment (noise), perfectionism, crises, problems with work-life balance, etc. Several factors, like sustained pressure, which has its own implications, are responsible. If they are in a stressful situation by different strategies and approaches, stress management makes regular improvements to one's life. Stress management means avoiding stress through self-care and relaxation; controlling one's reaction to stressful situations as they arise. In people's lives, stress management is highly necessary for living a good life, having healthy relationships, and avoiding any adverse health effects. There are different models of stress management, each with distinctive examples of mechanisms to cope with or control stress.

Figure 1: mindyog.com

- **Importance of Stress Management**

1. **Enables greater motivation for workers:** Stress affects employee morale and therefore their job efficiency. Not only does it affect the individual, but also the business. Stress demotivates the employees of the company, which causes absenteeism and employee turnover to increase. One can raise employee morale by using strong stress management skills, which motivates them and keeps them focused on their jobs and results.

2. **In a stressful situation, improving efficiency:** When the morale of the worker is strong and the relationship with the workplace remains intact. It increases efficiency for workers. Also in the most difficult cases, there would be very little risk of customer dissatisfaction or bad decision making with the use of strong stress management skills.

3. **Enables one to lead individuals in challenging times:** They look for guidance and direction when workers feel pressure. By addressing their

problems one by one, some of the staff can seek support. You will be able to lead in difficult times by using strong stress management skills and accurately recognizing the stressful issues.

4. **Reduces prospects for disputes in the workplace:** Workplace conflict is very prevalent and arises due to disparities in beliefs, personalities, and elevated stress levels. It cuts bonds and weakens the society as a whole. Efficient stress management skills, however, avoid certain distractions, build teamwork and make life simpler for all.

Figure 2:thatmate.com

5. **Reduces prospects for immoral problems:** During periods of high stress, unethical problems frequently rear their ugly head. There have been occasions when this technique has been used by people for shortcut purposes. Individuals begin to blame games at that period and point fingers at others. Strong stress management abilities, however, provide ethics and stress workshops to decrease the likelihood of unethical activities.

6. **Improves the likelihood of reaching deadlines:** Depending on the source of a stressor, workers become overwhelmed as stress rises. As a consequence, they do not perform to the anticipated standard and miss deadlines. Nonetheless, strong stress management skills allow them to recognize the stressors before they become a problem and guarantee that

business can run smoothly.

7. **Improves communication processes:** There is a detrimental impact on communication when stress levels are high. Employees cannot discuss work between individuals. Alternatively, they hunt for administrators to address business concerns or issues. Efficient stress management skills, however, help to identify and solve a problem, which improves the communication process.

8. **Helps to smoothly run projects:** Stress and administration go together. When managing a project, one never knows when the feedback is delayed or not given by the vendor. These problems make it difficult to meet the deadline that is needed. Often, the project employee is held accountable and asked to deal with pressures and meet the deadline.

9. **Allows one team to develop:** When staff feel tension, they cannot focus on their job. Often, the team has no unity. When any of the team members comment on them, they feel annoyed. A circumstance occurs when an employee addresses his concerns and requires assistance to solve them. You will develop and unite the team by managing stress as a strategy and using productive stress management resources.

10. **Enables one to provide workers with space:** When workers are active in work and are constantly busy, they do not have time to rest and relax, which causes tension in turn. Using useful skills in stress management and giving workers room to take a rest or a break. Enabling workers to take a breather at work allows them to recover their energy and decrease the effects of stress.

11. **Assists in the performance assessment of workers:** Every worker has a different stress threshold. Stress variables may be explicitly correlated with job efficiency. It also helps to determine how well workers function inside the team. It's also measurable. Efficient abilities in stress management allow one to measure them and conduct their performance evaluation.

12. **Four A's of Stress Management**

When the capacity to cope is exceeded by stress, equilibrium in the mind and body needs to be restored. A powerful method to do this is stress management. The four A's of stress management are to avoid, alter, accept and adapt.

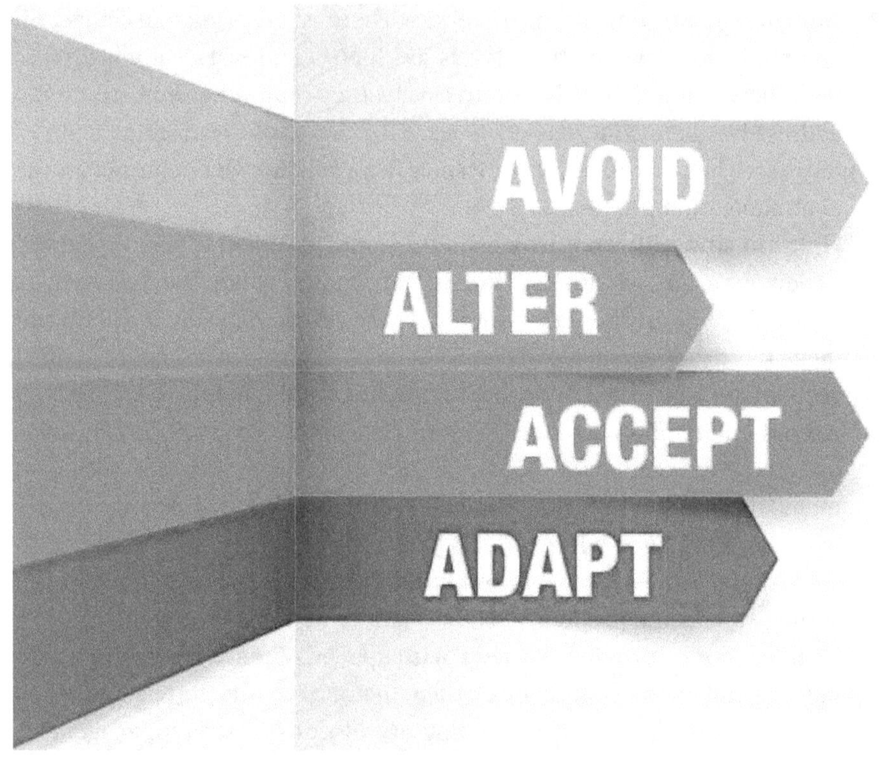


Figure 3: homework4.co.uk

1.**Avoid:** By planning ahead, rearranging workplaces and bearing a lighter workload, tension can also be stopped. The following methods include:

- Take charge: Taking control of stressful, repetitive assignments helps create trust. Leaving early for work or taking a different road, for example, will relieve the burden of traffic. The tension of standing in a line at lunchtime can be eased by planning lunch.
- Stop irritating people: anxiety can be relieved by physical distance from someone who is causing stress.
- Say "no.": There are a lot of commitments for most people and very little free time. It can be difficult to say "no" to social invites, additional duties at work or charitable requests, but it is also important for personal mental wellbeing."

- Prioritize a to-do list: Having a to-do list encourages the mind to let go of distracting thoughts about tasks needed. A feeling of satisfaction can be generated by scratching an item off the to-do list.

2. **Alter:** Attitudes, communication, and time management can need to be altered when stressful circumstances cannot be prevented. The following methods include:

- Ask others to improve their behavior: Small problems sometimes escalate and become big issues. It's all right to ask others to change disturbing behavior, but it's also necessary to listen to others about personal disturbing behavior.
- Openly communicate: The best policy is always sincerity. Using "I" statements rather than "you" statements when expressing feelings helps to negate any blame on the other person.
- Better time management: Grouping related tasks together will improve performance, resulting in reduced stress.
- State limits in advance: letting the other person know if time is short removes any bad feelings before engaging in a long discussion.

3. **Accept:** Acceptance is often the best way to avoid tension. The following methods include:

- Speak to others: Even though stressful circumstances cannot be modified, emotions are legitimate. It is good to address difficult situations with a friend who actively listens and understands.
- Forgive others: It takes practice to forgive. Learning forgiveness releases the mind and body from destructive energies.
- Practice constructive self-talk: Negative thoughts appear to feed off each other, producing extra negative thoughts. Positive self-talk can decrease tension and help keep objectivity going.
- Learn from mistakes: Errors are unavoidable and can be used instead of creating feelings of self-loathing as teachable moments.

4. **Adapt:** Adjusting also requires shifting perceptions, which in turn decreases levels of stress. This includes the following information:

- Standards adjustment: Perfection is difficult. Striving for perfection can trigger feelings of guilt and anger. Adjusting personal expectations will decrease stress.
- Practice avoiding bad thoughts: Negative thoughts should be substituted with positive ones immediately. In fact, refusing to replay a stressful situation in the mind can make it less stressful.
- Reframe the problem: It is always helpful to look at problems from a different angle. For example, use the day to catch up on television shows or read a book, rather than becoming upset by using a sick day from work
- Adopt mantra words: repeating confident phrases internally, such as, "I can do this," has a beneficial impact on stressful circumstances.
- Build a list of happy resources: It will put things in perspective to make a list of happy events, circumstances and feelings. In a stressful situation, looking back on this list will help relax the mind.
- Look at the big picture: It is important to find out whether anything would matter in one year or in five years. If it won't, tension can be relieved by letting it go.

**Recommendations**

Figure 4:psychologytoday.com

- **Get moving:** The last thing you really feel like doing is getting up and exercising while you're tired. Yet physical exercise is an enormous stress reliever, and to enjoy the benefits, you don't have to be an athlete or spend hours in a gym. Exercise releases endorphins that make you feel healthy, and it can also serve as a valuable diversion from your everyday concerns. While you can get the most benefit from exercising for 30 minutes or more on a regular basis, it is OK to gradually build up your fitness level. Over the course of a day, even very small events will add up. Having yourself up and going is the first move.

- **Connect with others:** Nothing is more relaxing than spending quality time with another human being who makes you feel comfortable and understood. Face-to-face interaction actually induces a cascade of hormones that counteracts the defensive "fight-or-flight" reaction of the body. It's the perfect stress reliever in nature (as an added bonus, it also helps stave off depression and anxiety). So, make it a point to communicate with family and friends on a regular basis and in person. Bear in mind that you don't need to be able to overcome the stress with the people you talk to. Simply, they have to be good listeners. And try not to let fears deter you from opening up about looking vulnerable or being a burden.

- **Making time for fun and relaxation:** By carving out "me" time, you can minimize tension in your life beyond a take-charge approach and a positive attitude. In the hustle and bustle of life, don't get so wrapped up that you neglect to take care of your own needs. Include your daily routine of rest and relaxation. Don't make encroachment on other commitments. Whether it's stargazing, playing the piano, or working on your bike, make time for recreational activities that bring you joy. Relaxation methods such as yoga, meditation, and deep breathing stimulate the reaction of the body to relaxation, a state of restfulness that is the opposite of the reaction to battle or flight or mobilizing tension.

- **Better control your time:** Bad management of time can cause a lot of stress. It's hard to keep calm and concentrated when you're stretched too thin and running behind them. Stop planning back-to-back stuff or attempting to fit too much into one day. Create a list of things you have to do and, in order of priority, tackle them. Do first with the high-priority objects. Create a step-by-step plan if a big project seems daunting. Instead of taking on all at once, concentrate on one manageable step at a time.

- **Maintain a balanced lifestyle balance:** Well-nourished bodies are better able to deal with stress, so be conscious of what you are eating. The temporary "highs" of caffeine and sugar frequently end with a mood and energy crash. You can feel more comfortable and sleep easier by decreasing the amount of coffee, soft drinks, chocolate, and sugar snacks in your diet. A simple release from stress may be offered by self-medication with alcohol or narcotics, but the relief is only temporary. Your mind, as well as your body, is fuelled by adequate sleep. Feeling exhausted can raise your tension and it will irrationally trigger you to worry.

### Conclusion

Job stress management implies learning to treat situations differently but it also means learning how to treat oneself, understanding one's strengths, and making better use of one's personal skills. It depends not only on external circumstances, but on our way of perceiving and interpreting them, to know how to handle stress at work or in any professional and personal sense. One of the most significant things to understand is that we are not battling tension, we are handling it. Stress management becomes important as it helps a person break the grip on one's life that stress has. Stress can affect one's physical and mental health, so stress management helps one live a healthier life. Stress management leads to achieving the overall goal of a healthy life, with sufficient time for work, family, relationships, fun, and relaxation. It also offers the resilience to work under pressure and tackle head-on challenges.

# CHAPTER EIGHT

# Stress Management in Adolescents during COVID-19 Pandemic

**Introduction**

Ever since countries all over the world have gone into lockdowns due to COVID-19, educational institutes have been no exception. Students and teachers have come across the perennial struggles of having access to uninterrupted and seamless quality of internet connection. To this universal problem, India has been no exception. Students and teachers across the hierarchy of educational backgrounds have found themselves in the eye of a near meltdown of internet bandwidth in many places. This state of affairs is adversely pitting academic institutions, tutors and students in a race against time. At the same time, it is compromising on student's much desired academic progress. However, universities and schools can adopt smart solutions to overcome the disruptive distress of adopting the online mode of communication.

Today the whole world is facing the problem due to COVID-19 pandemic and lockdown. Present situation creates stress for everyone but it affected badly to our children especially adolescents and they find difficulty to manage stress. It is a great challenge for academician also to continue teaching learning process without any hurdles and tackles the problems and queries of adolescents. Stress has been viewed as a set of neurological and physiological reactions that serves an adaptive function. The response-oriented approach defines it in terms of person's reactions to functioning under stressful conditions. In the stimulus oriented approach, stress is considered inherent to events/situation, and physiological threat/harm.

Stress is thus an imbalance between an individual's perception of demands and his capabilities to meet the demands, whereas a stressor is the catalyst linked to this imbalance.

According to Lazarus and Folkman (1984), the way an individual appraises an event plays a fundamental role in determining not only the magnitude of the stress response, but also the kind of coping strategies that the individual may employ in efforts to deal with the stress. Stress arises only when a particular transaction is appraised as a stressor. It must be personally relevant and there must be a perceived mismatch between a situation's demands and one's demand one's resources to cope with it.

The definitions of stress are galore. B.L. Seaward (1997) defined stress as "the inability to cope with a perceived or real threat to one's mental, physical emotional well-being which results in a series of physiological responses and adaptations." According to Cordon (1997), the term stress has been used to describe a variety of negative feelings and reactions that accompany threatening/challenging situations. Dunham (1984) defined stress as a process of behavioural, emotional, mental and physical reactions caused by prolonged increasing new pressures which are significantly greater than coping resources.

The orientation towards stress research is changing as awareness of the social and cultural context involves in stress, might be that "stress is a set of neurological and physiological reaction that serve an adaptive function in the environmental social and cultural values and structure within which the individual acts upon."

Perhaps the most important bit which is closely related to online education is that it can have psychological fallout of making adolescents feeling excluded and secluded. Adolescents may feel that they're lacking discipline and perhaps being below par, which could trigger anxiety. To beat this sense of frustration and lack of self-efficacy students require self-assurance and a reminder that they are not alone in this and will be able to come out knowing as much as other peers. Second and most importantly is that families and friends need to come closer for adolescents to provide them with needed psycho-social and knowledge-based support. This will ensure that adolescents are able to have a fulfilling academic experience through online education and by being at home during this novel time. As a former graduate of an online university and a frequent online-education beneficiary, the experience of online-education is second to none for all the right reasons, provided that there is drive, determination and devotion on part of the learner to keep learning and staying committed to time-bound goals.

**Sources of stress**

Adolescents suffer from stress even more than adults do, as they are exposed to new and confusing environments constantly. Their sense of self-worth is intimately tied to the expectations posed by the adults around them, such as parents and teachers but can also be influenced by their peers.

Due to COVID-19 lockdown, adolescents face lack of social interaction, physical activity, external exposure, and cognitive stimulation. That's why sometimes it is observed in them emotional outbursts like anger, sadness, irritability, crying spells, jealousy, fear of stepping out or interacting with others, not obeying elders, bad mouthing and fighting attitude, breaking objects around the house, hitting someone and yelling. Sometimes their behaviour also changes like lack of sleep or excessive sleep, lack of appetite or increased appetite, lack of energy, lethargic, clingy, staying separated from family, socially withdrawn, inattentive, academic downfall, loss of interest, physically weak or self harm and struggling to conduct simple activities. A person experiences stress when they perceive the demands of the environment to be greater that their perception of their ability to cope. These demands come in many shapes and forms. We make demands on ourselves, other people make demands and abilities and on our time, and life events are ongoing. In addition, there are numerous daily hassles such as overcrowded public transport and concern over money etc.

- **Family:** Hill (1970) showed that kinship bonds are very influential, resilent and are not dependent upon reinforcement. Therefore high levels of stress may be experienced but the relationship will continue and not end.
- **Personal and social issue:** Several studies have shown that people who experience many significant life changes are more susceptible to physical and mental illness. Holmes and Rahe (1967) developed the social Re-adjustment Rating Scale (SRRS) that scores major life events and changes according to their psychological impact. They found that higher scores on the SRRS increase the chances of developing stress-related illness.
- **Examination:** Much psychological research has focused on the stress accociated with examinations. For students in schools and colleges, test anxiety and distress constitute the near universal experiences, because

of the high test consciousness pervading the modern educational system (Humphrey, 1988).

- **Daily hassles:** According to Kanner et. al. (1981) it is daily hassles, rather than major life events, that aare stressful. They have developed the "hassel scale", a 117-items questionaries that is used to examine the relationship between hasseles and health. High scores on this scale have been found to be related to both physical predictor of ill health than high scores on the SRRS measuring stressful life events.

- **Workload:** Occupational overload comes from working ambience in one is faced with time pressure, excessive and diverse responsiblity and accountablity. Often there is lack of managerial or subordinate support, excessive role expectations from oneself or from one's superiors or others, so that task overload comes when the working environment places demands upon beyond one's available resources. Research seems to indicate that many jobs are deemed to be more stressful than is healthy for the employee. This is especially true of increased organizational accontablity. Academic overload comes when teachers experience increased responsibilities and then face increasing classroom violance, all the same time.

**Effects of stress:** Stress can affect us physically, emotionally, behaviourally and mentally.

**Physical:** Adrenalin is released into the blood stream. The heart rate and respiration increases. Muscles become tense; **Emotional:** Many feel irritability, anxiety, depression; **Behavioural:** Some experiences stress as a loss of physical co-ordination and control, lose sleep or act irrationally and **Mentally:** Stress can also reduce one's ability to concentrate process and store information in memory and solve mental problems.

**Stress management**

During counselling of adolescents, it is observed few changes in their behaviour such as alterations in cognitive functioning like memort deterioration, academic downfall, decrease in learning speed, poor in decision making, inability to solve complex problems, facing language problem in verbal and non-verbal communication, anxiety and depression.

That's why Periodical stress management programmes is needed for reducing the levels of stress among adolescents which in trun will improve their functional skills and lead to effective learning. The term "stress management" or "coping" have been used synonymously to denote the way of dealing stress, or the effort to "master" conditions harm, threat or challenges caused by stress.

**Coping styles:** It embodies physiological, cognitive and managerial styles of coping.

- *Physiological strategies*: characterised by some form of physical activity to distract or isolate oneself physically or mentally from the work environment.
- *Cognitive strategies:* Referring to the positive and supportive philosophies of life which are used to mentally cope with the tension of day-to-day activities.
- *Interpersonal and management strategies:* Referring to coping through use of principles, skills and techniques at work which enhances the feeling of being in control of the situation.

## Conclusion

Thus to avoid the negative effects of stress on adolescents, we should give appropriate amount of attention and spend quality time with them. We have to be aware of our children emotional and physical needs, always make our interactions intellectual, keep them updated. We should educate them about the current scenarios, provide them with adequate affection, exposure to the outside world, maintain a time-table, limit passive activities such as screen time, and conduct activities such as cooking, indoor games, extracurricular and cognitive activities. Work on reading skills to increase vocabulary and develop language, celebrate birthday and festivals and be mindful. In this way we keep our adolescents in good mental health and stress free. Because good mental health and stress free environment help our adolescents to reach developmental and emotional milestones, to learn healthy social skills and how to cope with problems.

# CHAPTER NINE

# Stress Management & Life Skills Development

**Introduction:**

Pressure cooker cooks 'dal-chawal' (pulse-rice) exceedingly fast due to pressure. Coal and Diamond score differently in their market values due to a little more 'pressure' that diamond could bear. It is this pressure that makes the crucial difference. Life examples are many, yet the society looks at stress with apprehension. One thing we must understand is that stress is an inescapable reality of life which cannot be wished away. Although it is customary to label the present times as stressful time yet the fact is that stress has always been there. The cave dweller faced stress from nature and other uncertainties that was a part of life then. So they had more stress because they were facing more uncertainties and the adage 'little knowledge is dangerous' sums the predicament rather aptly.

But in the present times with more knowledge and technology to support and predict environment, things seem to get worse. So, more knowledge has become more dangerous. Stress will always be a part of our lives. Wanted or unwanted, it is bound to come to us, from anywhere from everywhere. The question arises, whether to live with it or to avoid it? This may be a matter of debate but the best solution as indicated by experts appears to be development of stress tolerance because avoidance is more stressful and even otherwise it is practically impossible in any scenario, home or office!

Let us begin with a definition of Stress. Although there may be hundreds of ways in which stress can be defined, yet the one most widely accepted definition is given by McGrath. The definition says that stress is the perceived substantial imbalance between environmental demands and response capabilities and perceived important consequences of being not able to meet those demands. The focus on the word 'perceived' is crucial and suggest that stress is not usually 'out there' but 'in here'. So we understand why it is important to develop stress tolerance. It is the coping that does the trick and this coping can be learnt and developed.

**Nature of Stress**

Stressors could be internal and external both – Internal relate to anger, frustration, guilt, phobia, worry, uncertainty, novelty or even cultural shock that one might get in a particular situation; external relate to both family as well as office or workplace, there could be problems arising out of relationships (of different nature), competitive ambience, visual noise (thanks to our modern day gadgets) or even information overload, even aspirations! Being lonely could also lead to stress. Squabbles with friends may also result in stress.

There is need to understand that stress is not always bad. Stress that arouses you to accomplish a challenging task may, in fact, do a lot of good for performance enhancement. This is eustress. However, when this eustress exceeds an individual's tolerance capacity, it becomes distress which is harmful. Distress leads to negative implications and become worse when people try to avoid it.

A very high or a very low level of stress affects the mental and physical health of an individual. It can manifest as anxiety, aggression, irritability, dependency, withdrawal or depression leading to poor health conditions, inferior productivity and reduced morale. Moderate level of stress motivates and improves performance. Maintained at this level, stress is somewhat 'stimulating'. The principal strategy in fighting stress is neither to deny the existence of stress nor to be let down by it. The trick is to understand that it is a part of life and has to be conquered.

Usually, stress emanates from four sources – job characteristics, lifestyle, personality and support system. However, job characteristics and support systems are fairly stable and the incumbent may not be in a position to change them. Lifestyle and Personality can be altered with training the mind to reorient attitude and thought process. Perhaps, this is a reason why medical science today acknowledges the role of lifestyle and personality in disease origination and even cure. Managing life has become a critical issue now and they occur primarily due to three reasons – Hurry, Worry and Curry!

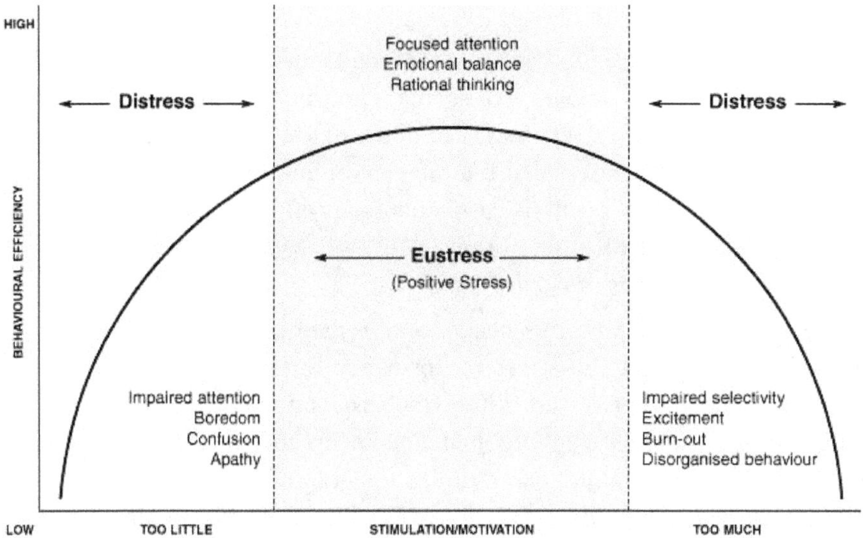


Stress is said to be a silent killer and has already emerged as a big social problem. It is the most mysterious of mental states. General strategies to manage stress include Reflection and Self-talk. Assertive behavior is yet another way to manage stress. In fact it is said that you have to take bull by the horns. The more you run away, the more it will bother you. Another issue is mismanaging time. Rather ironical that time is the most valuable resource that people have yet it is utilized in the most cavalry fashion.

Learning time management skill is one of the biggest ways to counter stress as of modern times. The way to react also offers some relief on this count. The feasible solution is personality restructuring – important components being Self Awareness, looking inside, coming up with SWOC (Strengths, Weaknesses, Opportunities, Challenges) patterns or filling up the ability – aspiration gap. Being ambitious is good but we must remember that over ambition leads to disastrous consequences. Though quite a tedious job for any one learning stress management, the ability aspiration gap can be bridged by dreaming right and scheming right, i.e., efforts must match the requirements of the goal otherwise it results in frustration.

Targets or goals must be in tune with an individual's capability and this is one major issue these days when there is too much of information that fires desires. But it must be realized that desires must be reasonable and achievable.

**Theoretical Base**

There is also need to understand that stress performance links are rather intriguing while too low of stress may not be conducive to effective performance, too high stress may lead to breakdown or burnout syndrome. It is always moderate stress that is a catalyst for good performance. Further, over obsession with result is also counter-productive. This is what an important lesson of Bhagwat Gita is. कर्मण्येवाधिकारस्ते मा फलेषु कदाचन । मा कर्मफलहेतुर्भूर्मा ते संगोऽस्त्वकर्मणि ॥

Balance is critical and this needs to be remembered always. The figure given below explains the stress performance link. Management of stress requires development of life skills which is found wanting these days in most people. Actually the problem lies in assumptions of entitlement. People have started taking many things for granted and even the slightest disruption can result in severe disequilibrium resulting in distress. Life skills then need to be learnt and practiced.

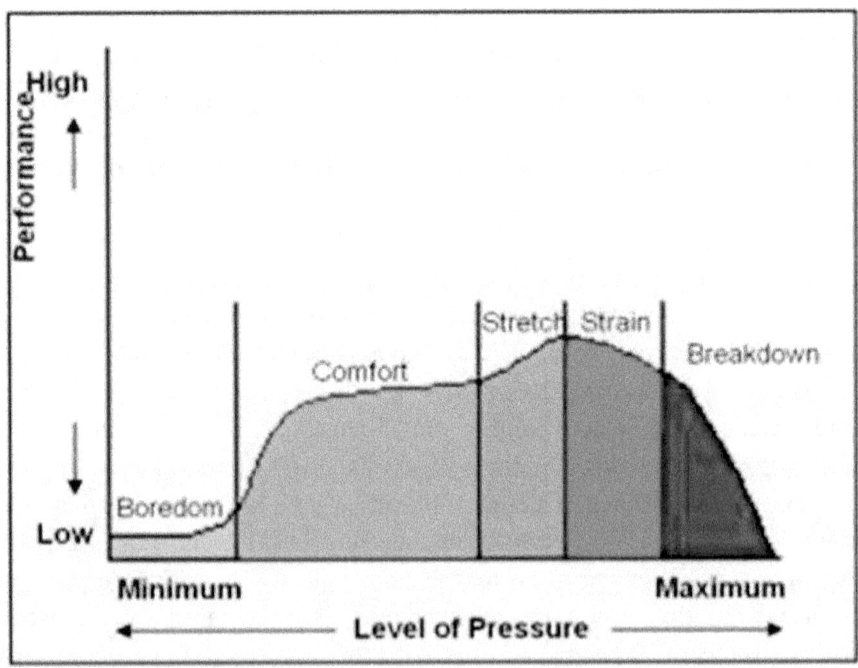

## Life Skills

Life skills are the beginning of wisdom which brings about behavioral change needed for a judicious utilization of attitude, knowledge and skills. Life skills enable individuals to translate knowledge, attitude and values into actual abilities, what to do and how to do it, given the scope and opportunity to do so.

Life skills are the abilities for adaptive and positive behaviour that enable individuals to deal effectively with the demands and challenges of everyday life. Adaptive here means that a person is flexible in approach and is able to adjust in different circumstances in different time frames. Positive behaviour implies that a person is forward looking and even in difficult situations, can find a ray of hope and opportunities to find solutions.

It is very clear that inner motivation reasons make a person work. Psychologically speaking this is intrinsic or self motivation. One cannot be pushed from behind or pulled from the front to do a certain task effectively. The drive has to come from within. As the adage goes, you can take a pony to the pond but cannot make it drink. It is based on the fact that we wish to do something because we desire for that, not because someone has told or wished! Observations in classical psychology suggest that around ninety per cent of intellectual capabilities are not utilized properly in most cases. Obviously, the effort-potential gap is immense and so also is the scope for improvement.

Knowing one self, changing one self and re-inventing oneself could be the way to mend such a gap. The SWOC analysis attempts to provide a framework for the same. Continuous improvement, multi-skilling and re-skilling or in other words consistent efforts in developing oneself may bring about a desired change in the way we take up challenges and thus ward off the threat of stress. There is need to attempt enhancing of productivity and competitiveness which subsequently will lead to capacity building. It has to be understood that beating one's own record is the time tested principle of excellence and it is rightly said that excellence is not a result, it is a habit!

It is imperative to train the present generation to develop a will for constructive use of time and resources and enjoy work rather than leisure. This will give a kind of positivity that helps in coping with stress by providing automatic resilience. This enhances capability to handle tough situations in life easily by utilization of mature minds and this can happen through thinking skills, social skills and emotional skills.

There are several life skills that need to be developed. Few important ones are Self-awareness, Empathy, Critical thinking, Creative thinking, Decision making, Problem Solving, Effective communication, Interpersonal relationship, emotional maturity. The authors would like to emphasize that emotional maturity holds the key and it can be nurtured by training.

**Stress Resilience & Management**

Simple steps for Stress Resilience include:

1. PROBLEM AWARENESS

Actually speaking, very few of us are able to realize what is causing stress. We tend to forcibly deny the fact of having stress to console ourselves; however, it slowly starts eating up the person's well-being without any realization. It robs us of the defense mechanism. It later develops into a vicious cycle where one stress (distress rather) gives rise to another adding to the persons' mental health. Hence, realizing the stress, its causes and finding ways to manage is the only solution, running away won't help in any case.

2. RELAXATION

Relaxing may reduce stress, idea being mind diversion to a different scenario which provides us with mental calmness. Although relaxation is an individual specific response, one has to understand that genuine relaxation must result in peace of mind. Watching television shows or listening to music or visiting some close friends or a power nap are substitutes available for the purpose. Relaxation not only subdues blood pressure and heart rate but also improves concentration, boosts up confidence and reduces anger and frustrations, all causes for stress.

3. EATING HEALTHY

In India, at least, mood is quite strongly related to food. We often say healthy mind rests in healthy body, hence, a healthy body happens to be relatively better equipped at handling stress situations. Our food intake determines what we are, how we behave or perceive how we wish to carry our lives – burdened or easy going! Certain types of food increase the tendency to become more aggressive whereas certain food catalyzes calmness and help in release of serotonin which is also known as "happy hormone". During stress, body releases cortisol into blood-stream which sends appetite-stimulating neurotransmitters into drive. This lowers the level of serotonin and programmes brain accordingly.

4. WORK-LIFE BALANCE

It happens to be one of the foremost issues addressed under different situations today, be it any work environment across the World. The moment we lose this balance, stress creeps in. Having passion for work or developing a tendency to be workaholic (deviating away from balance) may result in certain type of illness. Humans are social beings, they need to socialize and hence relax and hence maintain the desired balance.

## 5. PHYSICAL WORKOUT

Physically fit persons can manage emotional stress very well. Regular physical workouts decrease stress hormone cortisol and increases endorphin giving mood a natural boost. Moreover, during such physical sessions, the weird thoughts, stressors, do not bother us resulting in body and mind getting ample time to recover.

## 6. POSITIVE THINKING

Positive reference frame of mind not only creates better perception about people and situations, creates leadership quest but also helps in confidence pile-up rejuvenating life reducing stress, if any. This supported by a healthy diet and optimal physical workouts helps in coping with stressful situations better.

## 7. FOCUS ON SELF IS MUST

We do are a part of society and being in social groups is in our nature. However, at regular occasions, we need to be 'selfish', yes, taking out time only for ourselves, this helps in self introspection and finding out life anomalies that could be capturing stress. A regular break revitalize us and increases our capacity to handle life and work properly thereby managing stress.

## 8. ADEQUATE SLEEP

Sleep and mood are closely connected; poor or inadequate sleep can cause irritability and stress, while healthy sleep can enhance well-being. Chronic insomnia or sleeplessness may increase the risk of developing a mood disorder, such as anxiety or depression. Poor sleep and feelings of depression or anxiety can be helped through a variety of treatments, starting with improved sleep habits, and, if needed, extending to behavioral interventions and an assessment for a sleep or mood disorder. Irregular and disturbed sleep often hampers concentration and decreases energy levels. This in turn affects the effectiveness of work and increases stress. During sleep, the body rests, repairs, rebuilds, grows, and heals itself and stresses and tensions accrued throughout the day are ideally released.

## 9. PRAYER / MEDITATION / SPIRITUALITY

Both prayer and meditation work wonders in plummeting stress. Spending a few minutes in meditation can restore calmness and inner peace thereby balancing emotional well-being and the overall health. However, effective praying or meditation needs to be learnt through training. Both prayer and meditation require full concentration of an individual who needs to focus all his attention and get rid of the accumulation of insignificant things that trouble him in his in daily life. This helps in looking at the bigger canvas. Practicing spirituality can also offer soothe during stressful situations. The peaceful time spent during meditation or prayer gives our body and mind important time to relax and refresh. It helps lower heart rate, breathing rate and blood pressure. It helps in distancing from the distresses of life to a more peaceful and serene state of mind. This in turn rejuvenates an individual enhancing his/her stress tolerance.

## 10. TIME MANAGEMENT

It is one of the most important skills to possess in any circumstance or situation. One, who possesses this, perhaps is the richest person in 'peaceful' life terms. This skill is the most critical for effective stress control. Individuals should learn work prioritization; never commit the undoable or zero-value time wasting tasks. Plan of the day (POD) is essential in being effective in time management.

**Conclusion**

Stress is a reality of life and has to be handled with care. Any mishandling can result in disastrous consequences. The best way to face stress is to take up the challenge and try to find solutions rather than brooding over the problems. The truth that people seldom realize is that human capabilities are immense only one must learn to harness them. As it is common knowledge that individuals differ in their stress tolerance capacity a solution can be to raise this capacity with a little bit of thinking and training.

# CHAPTER TEN

# Stress among Adolescents in correlation to Academic performance and Socio-demographic determinants

**Introduction**

Adolescents are the group that lies in-between the childhood and the adulthood phase where the behavior change, emotion as well as social status is a well-known phenomenon. Thus, the age group 10-19 years are demarcated as the 'transitional' phase (WHO 1995; Debnath et al. 2019; Bose et al. 2020) where different factors act as catalysts to overcome different stressful situations belonging to the academic fields or in the society in which they belong. Thus, the adolescent's phase is very sensitive where changes occur in both physiological and psychological factors where the responding capabilities differ from individual to individual. Stress during the growing period is the normal part where both negative changes, as well as positive changes, occur during the very phase. Teenagers are referred to as such a part of the population where the level of stress exists to a very high level and it's a difficult period to cope up with the outgrowing situation.

Stress as it has both the outcome in the hand that includes both the good side as well as the bad side there deals a various factor and causes for the outgrowth of stress. Academic stress to socio-demographic stress counts as a maximum outcome of causes and consequences leading to stress. Primary studies lead to secondary studies further proceeds to tertiary studies which lead to employment where life challenges occur from leaving school and entering college and then the further continuation of higher studies. The lack of time with unprepared maintenance which deals with the consumption of time further raises the pressure and anxiety for dealing with the situation. The commitment to educational development as well as extracurricular activities further results in achieving the required commitments thus, leading to stress. Stress among adolescence is found to be so much in proportional that affects the mental health and daily habits do reduce the amount of sleep. Lack of sleep or sleepless nights give rise to mental disbalance thus affecting the psychological as well as physiological growth of the adolescence. The change in behavior and attitude directs towards the experience of stress which causes situations such as getting panic, loss of concentration, bifurcations in attention span as well as disengagement towards various co-curricular activities.

Adolescence like to go out and stay with their peers, but a situation arises where they must stay at home for a longer time with the family members which further goes against their will which further rise in quarrels with parents where the situation arises to both irritability and emotional pressure does stress develops. This situation further rises in conflicts between the parents which slowly increases whereas during the same phase closeness among the bonds of friendship with the peer's increases (Hirvonen et al. 2019). The central nervous system or the CNS which comprises the brain has an implication of stress which relates to the physiological and psychological determinants which though affects the growth and development of the body further the association of the brain with stress is not clear. The adolescents as they show changes in their body development where pubertal maturation occurs at the peak, the development of stress is counted among the natural occurrence phenomenon, thus stress-related disorder is very much natural were anxiety, depression, sleeping disorder, drug abuse, sexual relationship, and emotional disbalance shows high prevalence as depicted in Figure 1. Stress is a public issue where each individual is grasped under the burden of stress (Lal 2014).

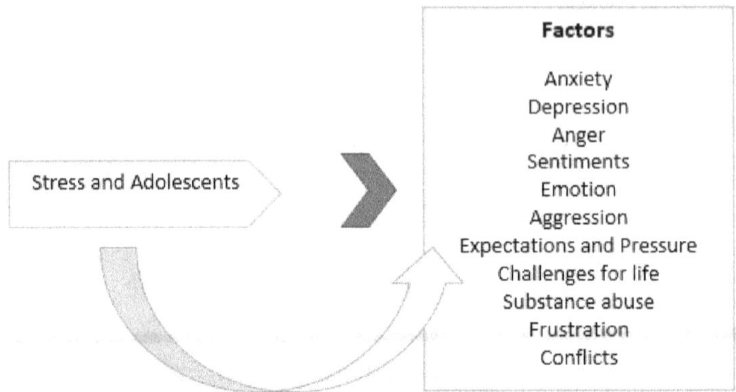


Hormonal influences trigger by the hypothalamus increase the level of stress among the transitional group.

Fig 1: The factors influencing stress among adolescents

The decision-making possibilities where rules and orders are to be followed in the social system where modernization and westernization are followed, the adolescents face problems in their surroundings which includes educational settings, economical and financial crises which effects the thinking capabilities and the lifestyle patterns (Lal 2014). The various signs and symptoms which make an increase in stress level are an increase in cardiac rhythm, increase in the level of blood, fatigue, tiredness, increase in cramps, muscle disorientation, diarrhea, blockage in the respiratory passages, and restlessness. The behavioral changes encompass the consumption of drugs, alcohol, cigar, and tobaccos. The eating habits further can depict the stress as obese or overweight adolescents when faces stress eat in excess whereas undernourished adolescents eat less which shows a loss in appetite (Lal 2014).

**Hormone, Stress, and adolescents**

The pubertal changes among adolescents are at a peak during these phases where there lies a direct relationship to the growth and development of the body. The hormonal changes play a vital role during the ongoing transitional phases where peak shift occurs in the hypothalamus region proceeding to the adrenal gland and the pituitary gland. These endocrine glands secret specific hormones which further induce the stress response in terms of various factors such as depression and anxiety. The hormonal change during this phase affects the development of the brain which is the main component of the central nervous system. The neural development and the maturation phase change with repetitive exposure to stress where sensitivity towards the dysfunctional phenomenon leads to maladaptive behavior. The continuity of stress for a longer period affects the cortical, limbic as well as lumbar regions of the body. The outcome of stress diminishes the normal growth where the 'neurobehavioral' function deteriorates (Romeo 2013). Hormonal response to stress serves as a quick action that affects the physical and psychological factors. The immediate responsive system of the body which performs the rapid reaction chain system consists of the sympathetic nervous system where stress triggers the release of both epinephrine and norepinephrine. This depicts the 'fight-or-flight' responsive character to minimize stress among the growing adolescents (Romeo 2013). The hypothalamus-pituitary and the adrenal gland initiate the response to hormonal release where corticotropin-releasing hormone from the hypothalamus region of the brain triggers the release of adrenocorticotropic hormone from the pituitary gland which further increases the stimulation of glucocorticoids from the adrenal gland. The hormonal regulation further is responsible for the increase in stress level thus contributing to the dysfunction of the immune system and reactions. The learning capabilities decreases which further reduces the attention span, mental capabilities as well as diminishes the Intelligent Quotient (IQ). The hormonal misbalance shows adaptive deterioration in cognitive development which influences the impaired response mechanism in the developmental phase of the growing adolescents. The stress-related response serves as an effective cause that bifurcates into both long-term to short-term effects, thus resulting in maladaptive behaviors. The earlier stage of adolescents including the age between 9 to 13 years of age shows low cortisol level induced stress adaptation than the later adolescents phase of 15-17 years of age (Stroud et al. 2009; Romeo 2013).

Hypothalamus secretes a corticotropic-releasing hormone that triggers the pituitary to release adrenocorticotropic hormone or ACTH, which further stimulates the adrenal glands to release glucocorticoids.

The sympathetic nervous system releases epinephrine and norepinephrine which severs as the immediate response to stress.

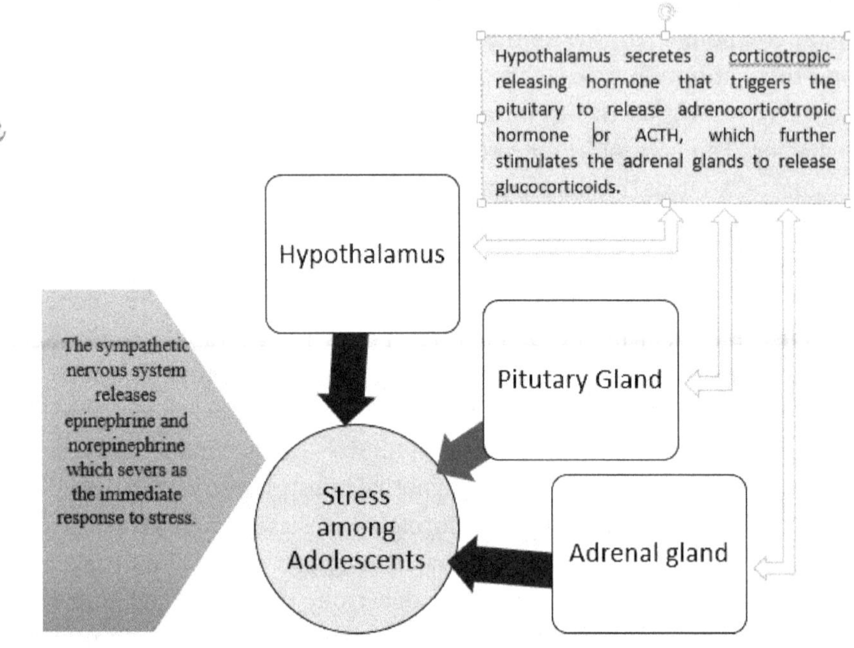


Figure 2: The hormonal regulation in the context to stress among adolescents

## Academic performances and Stress among Adolescents

Adolescents are the period that is among the largest group of the population worldwide. This period undergoes different physiological and psychological development which results in the development of stresses which bifurcates into various fields which include the academic field as one of the important fields were competition, pressure, emotion, and performance serves as an important determinant which tackles the prevalence of stress. Education is very important and it determines the future of the adolescents group so stress is also seen to occur among the group in both severe to moderate form. Stress among adolescents starts from the very early phase as in case of examination were performance matters both in formative as well as in summative examination thus competition develops among the peers were higher or lower marks in comparison to their peers' results in developing high stress were mental health also plays an important role towards the increment in stress.

The teacher-student relationship interacts with the perceptional changes among the adolescents where emotional and performance relate with each other further experiencing academic stress. Academic stress has a direct relation with the parental generation which directly affects the academic performance level (Luo et al. 2020). A study by Luo et al. 2020 included 1214 students from Xi'an, China, where parent's emotion was tested showing lower emotional stress among middle-aged students' relation with academic pressure. Academic stress was also studied by Huan et al. 2008 where adolescents stress was measured using various criteria which encircled the school, family, oneself, and the peer groups. The study showed the difference in stress distinguishing the gender differences were girls showed a high increase in the level of stress while competing in the school-related field, which further showed that academic stress differs among the boys and the girls where girls are found to be severely affected. Individual beliefs and challenges in the academic fields threaten the commitments to achieve the desire goals. The situational experiment to achieve the goals among adolescents vary accordingly where some take it as a challenging situation and proceeds to the 'try again' situation giving it a second chance whereas others may take the situation as a threatening or demoralized situation further losing all hope to succeed. A very recent study by Rentala et al. 2019 where 314 adolescents girls were studied. The study showed an association between educational stress and various socio-demographic factors. 63.5% of Indian students develop stress due to high academic pressure (Deb et al. 2015). A study in Thiruvananthapuram, India shows that more than 93% of stress develops due to educational performance. Academic stress develops a correlation between mental health and the formation of depression strategies. Adolescents girls are more subjected to a high level of stress than boys as the stage and level of worries differentiates among the gender. The formation of negativity in contrast to intrapersonal and interpersonal events is the cause of more stressfulness among the girls (Washington 2009; Anniko et al. 2019). Jayanti et al. 2015 studied the relationship between academic stress and the level of depression among 1120 adolescents in Tamil Nadu, India where a higher level of association between depression and stress was observed among adolescents in the academic field than the ones who were not in the academic field.

**Socio-demographic determinants that contribute to Stress**

The society in which one belongs or the habitat in which one resides is a very important output in contrast to the rise or fall in the level of stress. The family is the primary group that inculcates the mechanism in controlling the stress among adolescents. Parents are the important role model for their growing teens where behavior, attitudes, as well as emotional well-being, directly affects the signs of stress among the very group. The high expectations and the creation of extra pressure to perform well in all fields which includes both life skills as well as academic fields are the results of a significant increase in the stress level. The relationship with the peers which includes the relationship of love affairs further changes the social relationship to such an extent that the teenagers during this phase develop the stress level to the severe stages. The broken relationship and further mending it to the previous forms are the cause of stress. Teenagers are often given pocket money for their commitments whereas there are families who cannot afford the same which further give rise to bullying and teasing from the teenagers who receive so from their parents thus giving rise to negativity and leading to depression and emotional disbalances.

Huan et al. 2008 when studied academic performance considering various factors among the adolescents group the level of stress among both the girls and the boys showed similarity in case of personal causes, which include the family as well as the peers. The socio-demographic factors such as the residential areas in which an adolescents belongs, the type of religion, educational qualification of the parents, occupation of the parents, family type, birth order, and the number of siblings show a close association with the level of stress (Rentala et al. 2019). Literacy levels among the parents exhibit optimum to a high level of stress where illiteracy among parents shows high positivity towards the development of stress. Birth order and size is a very important factor as many siblings to the number of births highly correlates to the accommodation of stress. Further higher stress affects the nutritional status of the growing adolescents. The nutritional status diminishes the health of the individual resulting in malnutrition. The various occupation categories are related to the income of the family where moderate to high income reduces the level of stress as the adolescents can fulfill their required needs whereas low-income families cannot facilitate the fulfillment of needs among the adolescents thus developing the emotional and psychological pressure leading to stress. Thus, teenagers are facing various challenges where the society demands various roles from them, which is in terms of both defined and undefined, consistent to inconsistent, achievable to unachievable contexts resulting in the development of stress (Lal 2014).

**Conclusion**

Adolescence and stress can be used together as this is the very group that possesses maximum stress. Stress though having both positive as well as negative causes it shifts towards the negativity much more than the positive causes thus, teenagers can harm both growth and development as well as can severely affect the health as well as the mental wellbeing of the individual. The family plays a very important and vital role in minimizing the stress among adolescents as they stay the maximum time with them when remaining indoors. The academic performance, as well as the school activities which includes both the educational as well as co-curricular fields, should be thoroughly monitored by the teachers in the school so that the adolescence who have been under the consequences of stress for a longer period should be thoroughly monitored. Policies should be adopted so that the adolescence should be allowed to talk about the difficulties they are facing. Various interventions should be held so that stress can be minimized whereas schools should hire counselors for the process of monitoring the level of stress among the growing adolescence. This would further help both the parents as well as the school academicians to understand the level of stress for every adolescent facing which would further help and allow talking about the matter and provide a solution to it.

**Conflict of Interest:** The authors report no conflict of interest. The authors alone are responsible for the writing content of the paper.

**Acknowledgment:** Authors gratefully acknowledged the Department of Anthropology, University of North Bengal, and Ishwar Chandra Vidyasagar High School for extended help and co-operation.

# Bibliography


- Anniko, M.K., Boersma, K., Tillfors, M. (2019). Sources of stress and worry in the development of stress-related mental health problems: A longitudinal investigation from early-to mid-adolescence. Anxiety Stress Coping, 32:155–67.
- Bose, A., Sinha, I., Lata Tigga, P., Mondal, N., Sen, J. (2020). Socio-economic and Demographic Determinants of Double Burden of Malnutrition among Rajbanshi School-going Children aged 9-14 Years from North Bengal, India. Antrocom J. of Anthropology, 16(2):141-152.
- Adelina, Broadbridge (2000). "Stress and the Female Retail manager", Women in Management Review, Vol. 15, No. 3, pp. 145 – 159.
- Alexandros, S. G. A., Marilyn, J. D., & Cary, L. C. (2003). "Occupational Stress, Job Satisfaction and Health State in Male and Female Junior Hospital Doctors in Greece", Journal of Managerial Psychology, Vol. 18, No. 6, pp. 592 – 621.
- Andrew, J. Noblet, & Sandra, M. Gifford (2002). "The Sources of Stress Experienced by Professional Australian Footballers", Journal of Applied Sport Psychology, Vol. 14, pp. 1–13.
- Aniza, I. M. H.; Malini, R. M. & Khalib, L. MPH (2010). "A Study on Organizational Factors That Influence Job Stress Among Medical Laboratory Technologists in Klang Valle y Hospitals", Med J Malaysia, Vol. 65, No. 2, pp. 103 – 107.
- Coetzer, W. J. and Rothmann, S. (2006). "Occupational stress of employees in an insurance co mpany", South African Journal of Business Management, Vol. 37, No. 3, pp. 29 – 39.
- Daisy, Chauhan (2006). "Managing Stress: An Integrative Approach", Journal of Productivity, Vol. 47, No. 3, pp. 223 - 231.
- Lakshmi, Narayanan, R. (2006). "An Overview Of Strategic Planning To Combat Occupational Stress – Need Of The Hour In The Present Indian Context", National Institute of Virology, Indian Council of Medical Research, Pune, Maharashtra.
- Michailidis, M. & Georgiou, Y. (2005). "Emplo yee occupational stress in banking", Work, Vol. 24, No. 2, pp. 123 – 137.
- Mohsin, Aziz (2004). "Role Stress among Women in the Indian Information Technology Sector", Women In Management Review, Vol.

19, No. 7, pp. 356 – 363.

- Moustaka, E, Antoniadou, F, Malliarou, M, Zantzos, E. I., Kiriaki C, Constantinidis T. (2010). "Research in occupational stress among nursing staff - a comparative study in capital and regional hospitals", Hellenic journal of nursing studies, Vol. 3, No. 3, pp. 79 – 84.
- Muhammad, Iamal (1990). Relationship of Job Stress and Type-A Behavior to Employees' Job Satisfaction, Organizational Commitment, Psychosomatic Health Problems, and Turnover Motivation, Human Relations, Vol. 43, pp. 727-738.
- Roland, P. Chaplain (2001). "Stress and Job Satisfaction among Primary HeadteachersA Question of Balance?", Educational Management Administration & Leadership Vol. 29, No. 2, pp. 197-215.
- Shailendra, Singh and Aravind, Sinha (1986). "Stress at Work: Correlates of perceived time urgency and challenge in work", Psychological studies, Vol. 31, pp. 48 – 50.
- Deb, S., Strodl, E., Sun, J. (2015). Academic stress, parental pressure, anxiety and mental health among Indian high school students. Int J Psychol Behav Sci, 5:26–34.
- Debnath, S., Mondal, N., Sen, J. (2019). Double burden of malnutrition among adolescents in India: A Review. Hum Biol Rev, 8(2):155-178.
- Hirvonen, R., Yli-Kivisto, L., Putwain, D.W., Ahonen, T., Kiuru, N. (2019). School-related stress among sixth-grade students – Associations with academic buoyancy and temperament. Learning Individual Differ. 70:100-108.
- Huan, V. S., See, Y. L., Ang, P. R., Har, C. W. (2008). The impact of adolescent concerns on their academic stress. Educational Review. 60(2):169-178.
- Lectures on Homeopathic Materia Medica by James Tyler Kent
- New Manual of Homoeopathic Materia Medica & Repertory With Relationship of Remedies--By William Boericke
- Nash E. B.: Leaders in Hom. therapeutics
- Keynotes and Characteristics. by H C Allen.
- Gems: Textbook of Homeopathic Materia Medica: 1 Paperback – 7 June 2013 by J. D. Patil
- The Genius Of Homoeopathy: 1 Hardcover – 1 January 2008 by Close Stuart M.
- Jayanthi, P., Thirunavukarasu, M., Rajamanickam, R. (2015). Academic stress and depression among adolescents: A cross-sectional study. Ind

Pedtrics. 52:217-219.

- Lal, K. (2014). Academic stress among adolescents in relation to Intelligence and demographic factors. Amer Int J Res Hum, Arts Social Sci. 5(1): 123-129.
- Luo, Y., Deng, Y., Zhang, H. (2020). The influences of parental emotional warmth on the association between perceived teacher–student relationships and academic stress among middle school students in China. Children Youth Serv Rev. 114:105014.
- Rentala, S., Nayak, R. B., Patil, S. D., Hegde, G. S., Aladakatti, R. (2019). Academic stress among Indian adolescent girls. J Edu Health Promo. 8:158.
- Romeo, R. D. (2013). The Teenage Brain: The Stress Response and the Adolescent Brain. Curr Dir Psychol Sci. 22(2):140-145.
- Stroud, L. R., Foster, E., Papandonatos, G. D., Handwerger, K., Granger, D. A., Kivlighan, K. T., Niaura, R. (2009). Stress response and the adolescent transition: performance versus peer rejection stressors. Dev Psychopathology. 21:47-68.
- Washington, T.F. (2009). Psychological stress and anxiety in middle to late childhood and early adolescence: Manifestations and management. J Pediatr Nurs. 24:302–13.
- World Health Organization. (1995), Physical Status: The Use and Interpretation of Anthropometry. Technical Reports Series No. 854. World Health Organization: Geneva.
- Cooper Cary L, Sloan Stephen L and William S.: Occupational stress indicator. Management Guide, Nfer-Nelson Publishing Company, 1988.
- Greenberg J, Baron A. Robert: Behavior in organizations. Prentice Hall International, Inc, New Jersey, 2003.
- Pathak P.: Organizational effectiveness as a function of occupational stress and coping styles of executives in Indian coal industry – A case study, 1992; PhD thesis (unpublished).
- Albertson, L.M., and Kagan D.M. (1987). Occupational stress among teachers. Journal of Research and Development in Education, 21,69-75
- American Psychological association (1994). Publication Manual of the American Psychological Association (4th ed.) Wasington: DC, Author
- Blase, J. J. (1986). A qualitative analysis of sources of teacher stress: consequences for performance. Journal of American Educational Research, 23, 13-40
- Borg, M.G. (1990). Occupational stress in British educational setting: A

review. Educational Psychologist, 10,(2), 103-126

- Dunham, J. (1984), Stress in Teaching, New York: Nichols Publishing Company.
- Kanner, A.D., Coyne, J.C., Schaefer, C. (1981). Stress Management: daily hassles and uplift versus major life events. Journal of Behavioural Medicine, 4, 1-39
- Mangal, S. K. (2003). Statistics in Psychology and Education. New Delhi: Printice Hall of India Pvt. Ltd.


- Quick C, Murphy LR, Hurrell J. Jr.: Stress and Wellbeing at work. American Psychological Association, Washington, D.C., 1992.
- Tudu P. N., Pathak P.: Managing Employee Stress, Ways to minimize distress. Global Journal of Finance and Management, RIP, 2014, 6/5, pp 419-426.
- 11 Awesome Benefits of Importance of Stress Management in the Workplace, https://www.harishsaras.com/stress-management/importance-of-stress-management-in-the-workplace/, Harish Saras
- Stress_management_-reference_document-.pdf, https://ssq.ca/sites/default/files/archives/ac/Chroniques_sante/Stress_management_-reference_document-.pdf
- What Is Stress?, https://www.verywellmind.com/stress-and-health-3145086, Elizabeth Scott, MS, August 03, 2020
- Stress, https://my.clevelandclinic.org/health/articles/11874-stress
- UNDERSTANDING WORK STRESS: CAUSES, SYMPTOMS AND SOLUTIONS, https://online.csp.edu/blog/business/understanding-work-stress/, September 4, 2015
- Stress and achievement motivation: What are the effects of stress on achievement motivation?
- Theories of Motivation and Their Application in Organizations: A Risk Analysis, https://researchleap.com/theories-motivation-application-organizations-risk-analysis/
- Herzberg's Two-Factor Theory of Motivation, https://managementstudyguide.com/herzbergs-theory-motivation.htm
- Seven steps to help protect yourself from stress, https://www.mentalhealth.org.uk/publications/how-manage-and-reduce-stress
- Stress Management, https://www.helpguide.org/articles/stress/stress-management.

- PanigrahiAshok,Associate Professor, NarseeMonjee Institute of Management Studies, NMIMS University, Shirpur(Managing stress at workplace,Review article)
- Stress Management Essay | Essay on Stress Management for Students and Children in English, https://www.aplustopper.com/stress-management-essay/, Prasanna, January 15, 2021
- The 4 A's of Stress Management, https://www.painscale.com/article/the-4-a-s-of-stress-management, MedlinePlus, Mayo Clinic
- http://blog.readytomanage.com/stress-diagram/
- https://pramodpathak.com/2015/10/26/how-to-cope-with-stress/
- https://www.hseni.gov.uk/articles/what-work-related-stress
- https://www.betterhealth.vic.gov.au/health/HealthyLiving/work-related-stress
- https://www.good-thinking.uk/types-stress/
- https://www.mayoclinic.org/healthy-lifestyle/stress-management/in-depth/stress-relief/art-20044476
- https://www.ukessays.com/essays/psychology/stress-is-a-common-problem-in-modern-life-psychology-essay.php
- https://www.slideshare.net/mobile/sureshaadi0/stress-management-by-suresh-aadi8888-16309198